Freedom in Congo

CONGO, one of the world's largest countries which has shot into the headlines as a supreme example of how NOT to achieve Independence! CONGO, scene of strife, bloodshed and political intrigue, divided and harassed, the United Nations' biggest headache.

CONGO, land of innumerable tribes, languages and customs, with immense forests and

Yet CONGO i
world, to men and
freedom. The grea
significance in CC
restless peoples of t
Here is God's own
glorious freedom fro   , penalty and power of sin. Here is a body of mostly simple believers possessing no great educational or cultural advantages, but witnessing faithfully, suffering courageously and worshipping unitedly. For nearly one hundred years, missionaries have been penetrating to CONGO'S remotest regions, and the result is nearly a million naming the Name of Christ, in a population of 13½ million.

Kenneth Richardson knows CONGO as few people do. He has lived and worked for God among the Kakwa, Lugbaras and other tribes for more than thirty years. His son and daughter are both serving members, with their parents, of the Africa Inland Mission. As translator of the Word of God, evangelist and Bible teacher, pastor and administrator, Mr. Richardson has been serving CONGO'S peoples.

Latest statistics reveal no less than 32,000 Church Members, 4,200 of whom were baptised in 1961, shepherded by 103 ordained and licensed Pastors, within the field of the Africa Inland Mission alone. Roughly 600,000 different persons received medical treatment in the same area in 1961. Schools and training centres also are used by God to bring many to Salvation in Christ.

'FREEDOM IN CONGO' is a stirring book, to read prayerfully, an account for which every Christian will praise God.

FREEDOM IN CONGO

KENNETH RICHARDSON

Cover design by JOHN OLIVER

LONDON
PICKERING & INGLIS LTD.
1962

PICKERING & INGLIS LTD.

29 LUDGATE HILL, LONDON, E.C.4
229 BOTHWELL STREET, GLASGOW, C.2
Home Evangel Books Ltd., 25 Hobson Avenue, Toronto, 16

Made and Printed in Great Britain

Contents

CHAP.						PAGE
	INTRODUCTION	..	..	..	..	9
I	TWO BLACK EYES	..	..	..	..	11
II	EVANGELISM THROUGH EDUCATION				..	19

1 The Educational Ministry
2 Called by clothing
3 The beerpot which moved

III	DOCTORS AND WITCHDOCTORS		..	..	31

1 Medical Mission Work
2 Wizards that peep and mutter
3 A Tailor Turned ..
4 Freedom for the Chief
5 The Witchdoctor Doctored

IV	FROM SLAVERY OF SIN TO FREEDOM OF				
	SONSHIP	..	..	..	..	..	48

1 Faranka Moko
2 Goats, Grasshoppers and Grace
3 The Return of Dawidi Kaveve
4 Siku Moya
5 Can a Dead Man Save Others?
6 The Question which Persisted
7 Pagan to Pastor

CONTENTS

V   THE AZANDE TRIBE   83

   1   Fast Bound in Sin and Nature's Night

   2   Mbaraza

   3   The Hammer

VI   THE PYGMIES   98

   1   The Dwarfs of the Mountains of the Moon

   2   Reserved Accommodation

   3   As We Forgive

   4   Secret Idols

VII   HOW GREAT A MATTER A LITTLE FIRE KINDLETH   107

VIII   THE INDIGENOUS CHURCH   114

   EPILOGUE   127

List of Illustrations

MAP OF AFRICA INLAND MISSION CENTRES *Frontispiece*

Facing Page

AT THE COTTON MARKET   48

A CONGOLESE VILLAGER HANGS OUT
      MAIZE TO DRY   48

AFRICAN POLICEMAN DIRECTING TRAFFIC AT
      A BUSY CROSSROADS IN LEOPOLDVILLE   ..   49

THE MONUMENT TO STANLEY AND OTHER
      PIONEERS OF CIVILIZATION AT LEOPOLD-
      VILLE   49

A MODERN CONGOLESE HOME   64

CONGOLESE BUILDERS CONSTRUCTING A
      HOUSE   64

TWO LEADING CONGO PASTORS   65

A PYGMY IN CONVERSATION WITH A
      CONGOLESE OF ANOTHER TRIBE   65

Introduction

UHURU

The cry can be heard across the whole of central and eastern Africa. Sometimes it is given whimsically as a greeting. More often it is hissed out by envenomed lips against the European.

Uhuru! Uhuru! Uhuru! Freedom! Freedom! Freedom!

Yet how little the great mass of Africans understand what the freedom is for which they cry so impatiently, nor what to do with it when it has been granted. To many it speaks of freedom from all forms of restraint and law, from all authority. The result is that wise and kindly rules are trampled on and all forms of lawlessness manifest themselves.

Political freedom is a legitimate ambition. But the greater emancipation—freedom from sin, from fear, from superstition, from self—of which Africa, and all the world, is so ignorant, is offered freely, yet, all too often, not accepted. But those who are set free through accepting the Son of God as Saviour are 'free indeed'.

'Liberty to the captives and the opening of the prison to them that are bound' (Isa. 61. 1) is the promise of the Gospel for the sons of Africa as for all the sons of Adam. The Gospel knows no colour-bar in its application. In the following pages will be found stories showing something of the multifarious ways of our gracious God 'determined to save' and to bring the enslaved into the freedom of sonship.

CHAPTER I

TWO BLACK EYES

IF those two black eyes which opened recently on the strange Africa of today had opened years ago, how different the scene which would have confronted them!

Had they opened on the Central Africa of a century or more ago they would have seen both more and less than today. Less of civilization, but more of terror and fear. Many parts of the great continent were described on maps as 'unexplored'. Dean Swift tells how

> Geographers, in Afric-maps,
> With savage-pictures fill their gaps;
> And o'er unhabitable downs
> Place elephants for want of towns.

Inter-tribal and even inter-clan warfare was common, and this meant that every village had to be ready to defend its inhabitants against all comers. Not only so, but, from time to time, Arab slave-raiders invaded the countryside, killing, capturing, and deporting. Chiefs, in order to ingratiate themselves with the raiders, led forays against neighbouring tribes to gain captives for sale to them. Life was tragic. Life was hopeless. Life was uncertain. The people sacrificed to their ancestral spirits as they had always done, and have done since; but it was a gesture of hopelessness. It gave some comfort, but it was cold indeed, for the fetishes of the marauders were obviously stronger than those they themselves possessed.

Sir Philip Mitchell's description of the Africans of

Kenya in 1890 is equally true of all Central Africa at that time:

'They had no wheeled transport and (apart from the camels and donkeys of the pastoral nomads) no animal transport either; they had no roads, nor towns; no tools except small hand-hoes, axes, wooden digging-sticks and the like; no manufactures, and no industrial products except the simplest domestic handiwork; no commerce as we understand it, and no currency, although in some places barter of produce was facili-tated by the use of small shells; they had never heard of working for wages. They went stark-naked, or clad in the bark of trees, or the skins of animals, and they had no means of writing, even by hieroglyphics, nor of numbering except by their fingers or making notches on a stick or knots in a piece of grass or fibre; they had no weights or measures of any kind in general use. Perhaps most astonishing of all to the modern European mind, they had no calendar nor notations of the time, and reckoned by the moons and seasons and the rising and setting of the sun . . . They were pagan spirit, or ancestor propitiators in the grip of magic and witchcraft, their minds cribbed and con-fined by superstition . . . they are a people who in 1890 were in a more primitive condition than anything of which there is any record in pre-Roman Britain.' *The Agrarian Problem in Kenya.*

Yet even a century ago, there were the streaks of a great dawn, although their black eyes could not discern it. Livingstone made his great journeys be-tween 1850 and 1873. The famous statue overlooking the Victoria Falls portrays his rugged features as he strode forward in his travels, a walking-stick in one hand and a Bible in the other. As he explored the

Dark Continent he observed the damage caused by the slave-raiders. He found a society 'almost in dissolution and deeply wounded by its first contact with the outside world—the slave-trader.' He made it his objective to put down this infamous traffic, while at the same time bringing the way of release from that still more pernicious slavery of sin by the Gospel of Jesus Christ. He brought the first promise of Uhuru—Freedom.

About the same time Sir Samuel Baker discovered the lake which he named Lake Albert in honour of the Prince Consort of Queen Victoria.

Had those black eyes opened on the Congo of even eighty years ago, they would have seen but little of the dawn. Livingstone never entered the vast tract of country now called Congo; but he inspired Stanley, who made his long and arduous journeys, discovering the source of the Congo, and founding the Congo Free State.

Few people appreciate the vastness of Congo. An equilateral triangle with its angles on Paris, Riga and Athens would give some idea of its size, but a further triangle based on Paris-Riga would need to be added in order to include all Congo. Its area is approximately 925,000 square miles! The Coastline of Congo —only 25 miles in length—would be at Paris. Elizabethville would be at Athens, and the piece of territory where the Africa Inland Mission has been working— roughly the size of the British Isles—would be represented by Riga.

This huge area was once the personal possession of one man—Leopold II of Belgium. He took little detailed interest in it, and never visited it. Rubber and Ivory were State monopolies. Agents were inadequately paid, and in order to make their way, insisted that their African employees fill quotas of rubber. If they failed to bring in the required amount, they were mutilated or shot. Hands or feet, or both, were cut off. Bosses of labour gangs brought to their superiors baskets filled with hands hacked from those whose work had been insufficient. It was estimated that between five and eight million lives were forfeited at that time.

Yet the dawn was breaking, even in those days. For it was in 1878 that the first missionaries arrived in Congo—Protestants of the Livingstone Inland Mission. They were soon followed by others. And the black eyes which opened on the great world of lower Congo at that time could see something of the Great Light.

Fifty years ago! The opening black eyes of those days could see the beginning of many changes. Congo was no longer the property of one man. It had been taken over rather reluctantly by Belgium as a colony— a child nearly eighty times the size of the mother. Then conditions began to change. There was a new attitude towards the Africans, and as Lord Hailey suggests, the Belgian policy was based partly on 'the general determination that the rule of the colony should be such as to present the strongest possible contrast to the history of the Free State under Leopold II'.

Had the black eyes of half a century ago opened in Eastern Congo, they could have watched a small handful of missionaries climbing up the steep slopes above Lake Albert to establish the first station of the Africa Inland Mission in those parts. It was at Kasengu, among the Alur tribe. The mission already had work in what are now Kenya and Tanganyika. Before long, some of the party had moved further north, had entered the Azande tribe and settled at Dungu. Thus the dawn was breaking. The Gospel was beginning to give forth its rays on what had hitherto been unmitigated darkness.

Twenty five years ago! And the black eyes which looked out on Eastern Congo saw the way prepared for great progress. Mission stations had been opened at strategic points, and in the areas surrounding them, the Gospel was beginning to be preached by those who had just come out of the darkness and seen a great light. They had made their exodus from the captivity of ages and had entered into freedom. Hospitals had been opened, and doctors and nurses gave unstintingly of their time and strength to provide physical help and thus open the way for the preaching of the Gospel of Jesus Christ. Schools there were, too, primitive enough; but those who cared could learn to read and write. The desire for education had not yet become a craving, and the greater part of the pupils were those who had come to the Saviour and wished to be able to read the Scripture portions which had been translated for their help.

Those eyes would have watched as men and women missionaries ferreted out strange languages word by word, translated Scripture portions, tramped the countryside giving out the emancipating message, and poured out their souls in prayer for the people around —laying a good foundation for the years which have since intervened.

But the black eyes which open on the Congo of today see things of which their forebears never dreamed. Congo has broken from her chrysalis of darkness and ignorance and has emerged into the blinding glare of modern conditions. The criss-cross of bush paths which formed a network over the whole country has been succeeded by wide motor roads, along which travel all kinds of vehicles. The Belgians built huge modern cities and great airports. The air services which still link main points are piloted by Europeans, but nearly all the other transport is in the hands of Congolese.

The suddenness with which all this has come about has blinded the eyes of many of the people. In their bewilderment they are ready to heed any voice which cries, and to drink in any kind of propaganda, provided it comes—or professes to come—from African sources. That propaganda has turned against the Belgians and against Europeans in general, and, in consequence, the country has been denuded of those whose experience could have been of the greatest assistance in the running of the government, in the organization of transport and supplies. Moreover, it has undermined confidence in the United Nations also.

Sad Congo! The chaos and disorder which have come as the result of independence will take years to overcome, and may well be the country's undoing.

The great mass of people have no conception of the meaning of independence. The general idea is that it means freedom from all control or restraint. Many people have failed to dig their gardens or plant crops, believing that the government would provide them freely with food.

Yet amidst all the confusion and bewilderment, there is a body of people into whose hearts a new light has shined. Their hopes are not fixed on man, nor on political movements, but on God. They have found a freedom in Christ which cannot be obtained elsewhere. And although in the enthusiasm of political propaganda some of them suffer persecution, since they will not go to the same extremes as those who have no other loyalty, there are many who would rather die than give up their faith in Jesus Christ.

From the point of view of Protestant missions, Congo under the Belgians was run by a nation which was overwhelmingly Roman Catholic. The Colonial Charter promised that the Governor General would 'protect and favour, without distinction of nationality or creed . . . all religious enterprises.' But for many years it was impossible to obtain equality of treatment for Protestant missions; only after repeated representations by the Congo Protestant Council was this given. As recently as 1955 John Gunther wrote 'Three things run the Congo: Belgium . . . ; the Roman Catholic Church; and big business'—*Inside Africa.*

In view of this, the progress of Protestant missions in Congo is a modern miracle. With the ball heavily weighted against them, Protestants have gained approximately one third as many adherents as has the Roman Catholic Church. Moreover, Protestants have won for themselves a good reputation. Ordinary commercial firms hold them in high esteem as being sober and trustworthy. Speaking to the Congo Protestant Council shortly before Congo became independent, a high official said:

'It is impossible not to recognize how the majority of the Christians of your missions have made an impression on their neighbours by the dignity of their lives, their good daily conduct, and their respect for those in authority.'

The work of Protestant missions in Congo has been co-ordinated by the Congo Protestant Council, which has represented them before the Government. Under

God, the missions owe an enormous debt to this body. Through its good offices they have received the recognition which was their due, and have been given equality of treatment with the Roman Catholic missions. The Congo is almost unique in this respect that although there have been forty-four Protestant missionary societies at work—British, American, Swedish, Norwegian, South African, etc.—there is practically no overlapping.

CHAPTER II

EVANGELISM THROUGH EDUCATION

1. The Educational Ministry

WHY should evangelical missions engage in educational work? Do we not send out our missionaries to preach the Gospel?

These questions arise in the minds of many of the Lord's people, and some do not feel at liberty to support missions which follow an educational policy.

Whatever questions there may be in other lands regarding this matter, there can be little in Congo, for the following reasons.

(a) Practically all primary and secondary education in the Congo has been left in the hands of missions. The Government has done little along this line.

(b) Unless the Protestant missions provide for the education of their people, there was no alternative but that those who wished to learn should go to Roman Catholic schools. There they would not only be subjected to Roman Catholic propaganda, but cases have been commonly reported where pupils had been told that they would not be admitted to any but the lower classes unless they joined the Roman Catholic Church.

(c) As part of the official curriculum in the schools there is a daily period of Religious Instruction. In this the missions are given an absolutely free hand. The opportunity thus afforded of having so many of the rising generation under daily instruction in the Word of God for six days a week has provided an unparalleled opportunity. The saturation of the minds of the young in the eternal verities is not only productive of immediate results but leads also to more distant fruit.

(d) In Africa, as elsewhere, childhood has been found to be the most impressionable period of life, and the majority of conversions have taken place at that time.

Protestant missions were the first to engage in education in the Congo. This began with the desire that the people should be able to read the Word of God for themselves.

But for many years they laboured under a great handicap. An agreement entered into in 1925 between the Belgian Government and the Vatican gave the Catholic Church an absolute monopoly on State subsidies for education. Under this agreement, the Catholics received untold sums for their schools; but Protestant missions were left to struggle on with their own meagre resources. It was marvellous what they were able to accomplish. But it goes without saying that they were beaten in the race. It was only in 1948 that the Protestant missions were accepted on the same basis as Roman Catholics. Even since then, the Catholics having made such good use of the magnificent advantages given to them over more than twenty critical years, Protestant missions have never been able to make up the leeway.

When, after much prayer and hesitation, the Africa Inland Mission decided to enter the field of Government-sponsored education, it was felt wise to concentrate on teacher-training. It was hoped that the production of Christian teachers would, in time, take some of the load from the missionaries and at the same time provide for Christian teaching and influence in the schools—even if the mission schools were eventually taken over by the Government—by those who would use their vocation as an opportunity for evangelism.

But there were difficulties associated with this. Under the Belgian educational system, the future of the pupil has to be determined at a very early age, on the completion of his primary school education. While it is possible to judge a child's bent at the age of eleven or twelve, it is quite impossible to foretell what his spiritual standing or calibre will be. Missionaries and church leaders have done all in their power to ensure that only those who were spiritually fit were sent for further training along these lines; but it was impossible for them always to have unerring judgment. Many of those who have come out of our three teacher-training establishments in the A.I.M. are doing excellent work, and leading their pupils on in the ways of God. Yet there are others who have been rebellious and self-assertive, and have led their pupils astray. They need the prayers of the Lord's people.

Another question which presents itself to some is whether it is right for so-called 'Faith' missions, looking to the Lord alone for the supply of all that is needed, to take money from Government sources. This is indeed a large question, and much anxious thought was given to it. At length the decision was reached that the money should be accepted. A certain amount of the annual polltax paid by the Africans, goes to providing educational facilities. Unless the Protestant missions accepted their share of this money it would go to Catholic hands. Yet the Protestant adherents had paid their part of it, and felt that they had a right to education for which they had paid. And since, ultimately, education is a Government responsibility, it was felt that it was only right that state funds should be accepted by missions who were in effect helping the Government out.

This decision was reinforced by the fact that certificates issued by schools which were not subsidised, and therefore not recognised by the Government, were looked upon as valueless. So that graduates of non-subsidized schools have been refused recognition because their certificates were considered worthless.

There was still room for the exercise of faith, however, even when Government funds were accepted; for the grants given by the Belgian Government were well below the level of those given in British territories. There has always been a balance which had to be found by the missions.

2. CALLED BY CLOTHING

He had completed his first term at the little Protestant school, and was returning to his village for his first holiday. All eyes turned towards him as he approached.

'Ki!' said everybody in chorus. 'Ki!' and mouths were opened in astonishment, and hands were clapped over them.

The reason for the astonishment was not far to seek. The lad was wearing a pair of shorts!!! Shorts!!!

In common with all other Azande lads, he had never been seen in such apparel before. The usual dress was simply a piece of barkcloth as a loin-cloth.

Not that that is to be despised. It is produced locally. A strip of bark is gathered from the appropriate tree, hammered out on a piece of tree trunk with a special ivory-headed hammer, until it becomes a supple piece of light brown cloth.

But here he was, striding along with all the confidence in the world wearing a pair of shorts made from cotton material.

'Where did you get those shorts?' asked the other lads who crowded around him.

'The missionary gave them to me.'

'Why did he give them?'

'He gives them to all the boys who attend school.'

The lads fingered the material, and gazed on the garments admiringly.

'Does he give them to *all* who attend school?' asked one of the boys.

'Yes, everyone who goes to school and keeps on is given a pair of shorts like this.'

'Would he give me a pair?'

'Yes, if you went to school.'

So when the lad returned at the end of his vacation, he was accompanied by a new recruit.

A strange place, this mission station, thought the recruit. And strange people these Europeans.

He lived in a house with other schoolboys. Food was plentiful and some of their number were responsible for cooking and serving it. But he was amazed to find that none of it was offered to the spirits. Indeed, before eating, they all bowed their heads and thanked someone called God for providing it for them.

What sticklers they were for time, these missionaries! If you didn't rise in time, or get dressed in time, or go to school in time, or to work in time, or to bed in time, you were likely to be in trouble.

And cleanliness too! He couldn't see why they should be so particular that bodies were washed and kept clean; and that every day!

He didn't see how he could possibly be happy here,

However, he had a great desire to possess a pair of shorts. So he stayed on, and endured the unpleasantness.

'How long must I be here before I get a pair of shorts?' he enquired of one of the older boys.

'Maybe a week. Maybe two.'

Well, he would endure it that long, and when he had received the garment, he would run away to his home.

So he continued.

Day by day he attended school. For the first few days the strange marks which were displayed before him were utterly meaningless. Gradually it dawned upon him that they represented sounds.

Before many more days he had mastered the vowels. He then started on the other letters. As he mastered these, he was taught to link them up with vowels.

With great excitement he discovered one day that he was reading words which he could recognize. It was thrilling.

But he made other discoveries too. Day by day in school and at morning and evening prayers he heard of God, the great Creator of all. Almighty—mightier than the spirits whom he had learned to fear from his earliest days. Omniscient—wiser than Bengi who was consulted by all. And this wonderful Being was not only great and wise and just—but loving. Although people had turned away from Him and worshipped the spirits and done many wrong things, so loving was God that He had sent His only Son to die for sinful men. Those who opened their hearts to Him would be forgiven all their sins, and go to be with Him in His beautiful home for ever. Those who refused to believe in Him would go to a place of misery for ever.

These words made a deep impression upon him. He had the conviction that they were true. He could not yet come to the point of taking a definite step of committal, but he would like to hear more.

So it came about that when the great day arrived when he received the coveted shorts, he decided to remain at the mission rather than run back to his heathen home. It was not long before he reached the 'Happy day' that fixed his choice on Christ.

Life was different after that. He learned to pray about everything, and, in consequence, made better progress in school. Looking away to his Saviour he was able to overcome the temptations which assailed him on every hand on account of the loose morals of the tribe. He drank in the instruction which was given in the services and sought to conform to the will of God.

Came the day when an evangelist was needed to teach and preach at one of the posts away from the mission station. He was now a baptised member of the church, and had taken the name of Cornelius. As the need was brought to his notice he felt that the Holy Spirit was constraining him to respond. His offer was brought before the missionary and the elders of the church, and he was sent forth. The seal of the Lord's blessing was on his ministry and the centre to which he ministered grew, even though some of those interested found the demands of the new life too high, and they fell back into the old promiscuous tribal habits.

However, through blessing and discouragement, Cornelius carried on.

Not yet, however, had he taken a wife to himself. This he felt was not a step to be taken lightly. God who had planned all things for him, had designated the right helpmeet for him. He prayed that he might be guided to the right one.

The choice narrowed down to two. They were both Christian girls. One was about his own age. The negotiations would not take long, the bride-price could be paid quickly, and he could settle down to enjoy married life.

But as he prayed for direction, he felt drawn to the other girl. She was several years younger, resident in the Girls' Home on the mission station, and not yet old enough for marriage. He would have to wait several years for her, which was a great disadvantage. Nevertheless, during those years in the Girls' Home she would be gaining valuable preparation to be the wife of an evangelist.

To this one, therefore, he wrote a formal letter of proposal. It probably read something like this:

'Greetings to you in the Name of our Saviour who gave Himself to redeem us.

Are you well? I am well, as one may be in this world, sometimes well and sometimes ill.

I want you to be my wife. If you want me, reply to my letter quickly.

Many greetings, Cornelius.'

The girl returned a favourable reply.

Years later Cornelius confided to the missionary that the Lord had indeed led him to the right one. They had never once had any differences.

Cornelius has served faithfully and humbly as an evangelist for many years, but he has never had adequate training for the post. The education he had on the mission-station in those early days was very elementary, and far below the standard now demanded for primary education. All he knew of the Bible he had learned there and in the various Bible classes held on the station. He had read and re-read the portions of Scripture translated into his own tongue, and had become thoroughly familiar with them. But he could have benefited from further training. Again and again his name had been proposed as a candidate for the Evangelists' School. That would provide two years of Bible teaching. There was one difficulty, however, which always cropped up—his old father was quite blind, and was dependent upon him. So, in spite of his longings for a better understanding of the Word of God, he has not been able to have the advantage of the two years training.

His father has recently died, trusting in the Lord, and it is hoped that Cornelius may now be able to have further instruction.

3. THE BEERPOT WHICH MOVED

'All boys must enrol at the school'.

The order came from the Chief. Ever since the fall, an order of that nature has provoked a reaction of rebellion. This was the only school within a radius of many miles, and it had just opened. Education was a new thing, and at that time there was little desire for it. Little Danakpari, like a number of others, determined that he was not going to be tied to school. He did not want to learn to read or to hear of the religion the white people were teaching, and which the local evangelist was pressing on them.

The Chief sent his emissaries to the villages to search for boys who were not attending the school. Danakpari was still rebellious, however, and when he caught sight of the Chief's men he ran away to hide. But where could he go? Inside the house or granary he would soon be found. There was nothing behind which he could conceal himself. There was absolutely no hiding place—but stay! An idea suddenly came to him. Before him stood the huge earthenware vessels used for brewing beer. A boy could easily curl up inside one of them. So without delay he climbed up and was soon out of sight inside an empty beerpot.

Not a second too soon! The Chief's messengers came round looking for the truants. They searched the houses, the granaries, and anywhere else which might conceivably form a hiding place; but in vain. They would have to give it up.

They were just passing the beerpots, however, when one of them moved slightly, almost imperceptibly. The messengers stopped. What could have caused the movement? One of the men climbed up and peered in—and Danakpari was discovered.

And on that slight movement, the smallest of all hinges, a great door in the lad's life began to swing open.

Roughly they hauled him out of the pot, saying, 'Off to school with you'. They led him away to the Protestant school and delivered him to the teacher-evangelist.

Crestfallen, abashed, but still protesting, the boy took his place in the class. He was determined that he would not stay there for long. He waited a suitable opportunity, and then made a dash for it. Once again he was compelled to return. Again and again he ran away, and was as often returned.

But each time he returned he heard more about God from the faithful evangelist. God, the Creator of all things, had looked upon man whom He had created, had seen that he was ignoring God and worshipping spirits instead of God. That because of this and the fact that he was a sinner, God must punish him. But that God had so loved him that He had given His only begotten Son to 'bear the punishment instead'; that God was offering to him forgiveness if he would only accept this Saviour as his own. In the working of the Holy Spirit the truth began to make an impression which was deepened as the message was repeated. And eventually there came a happy day which fixed his choice on the Saviour.

Things were different from that day. The letters he had sought to remember but which had evaded him now stuck in his memory. Before long he was able to connect them up to form syllables and words, and then began to spell out the first sentences from the primer, and then, to his delight, he was reading for himself. That came after his conversion, when he prayed for divine help.

Having completed the first primer in the local school, he decided to go to the mission station (Dungu) where he could make further progress. He lived in the boys' home there, worked in the station gardens to produce his food, attended school and various meetings at which he learned more of the things of God. As time went on he joined a catechism class to prepare for baptism. The preparatory course lasts two years, after which, having been examined by the leaders as to their conversion, knowledge of the way of salvation, of the Scriptures and the catechism, and as to the evidence of change seen in their lives, they may be passed for baptism and church membership. On his baptism, Danakpari took the Bible name of Metusara (Methuselah).

The habit, usual throughout central Africa, of taking

a baptismal name from the Bible has its complications. At one time on our station so many had been baptised that the commoner names such as John and Peter and Matthew had been used many times, and people were beginning to take names of unknown people from the genealogies. These names were utterly meaningless. The next time there was a group ready for baptism I called them together and told them how ridiculous it was to take the name of somebody about which they knew nothing. They should select the name of a man with a characteristic they admired, and seek to emulate him. I was surprised to find that a number took the name of Methuselah—the man who lived the longest in Bible records.

So Metusara Danakpari progressed in the things of God, and as he absorbed more and more Bible truth he sought to translate it into daily life. Gradually, however, he came to see that this was not enough. He had a responsibility to those of his tribe who had not yet come to Christ. By this time he had married a Christian girl. Moved by the Holy Spirit, they offered to go out as evangelists. He was approved by the church leaders, and appointed to a bush centre to preach the Gospel and to seek, by conducting elementary reading classes, to lead the young into the ways of God, even as he himself had been led.

CHAPTER III

DOCTORS AND WITCHDOCTORS

1. MEDICAL MISSION WORK

Gardens are not made
By saying 'Oh, how beautiful' and sitting in the shade
While better men than we go out and start their working lives
At grubbing weeds from gravel paths with broken dinner knives.
Kipling

OUR God is One of infinite perfection. This is revealed in the wonders of the sky, the perfection of its timing and the precise balance of the physical properties involved. It is likewise revealed in the exact and infinite perfection of the minutest creation.

That our God can bring to pass His eternal purposes through frail and imperfect servants passes our comprehension and excites our admiration. Moreover our wonder is increased when those imperfect servants are inadequately and poorly furnished for the great tasks they have to perform. But so great is our God that not only does He choose the weak and despised instruments that His glorious power may be the better displayed, but it is often His good pleasure to permit those servants to lack much that might seem to be desirable in the way of equipment.

Those who associate medical and surgical work with gleaming tiles and polished steel under penetrating electric light would not believe their eyes could they have seen the crude conditions under which the doctors worked in the early days. A mud hut had to serve as operating theatre, calico draped above the home-made table to catch the stray pieces of dirt or grass, or the insects which dropped from the thatched roof. The only illumination was a hurricane lantern. Under these primitive conditions critical operations were performed. Yet the finger of God so wrought through these doctors and the nurses associated with them, that miracles were brought about.

Daring or foolhardy hunters followed hard on the tracks of buffalo or elephant they had wounded with their old-fashioned guns, and were often severely gored when the animals turned on them. People whose scalps and bodies had been torn by the claws of leopards, or whose legs had been horribly mutilated as crocodile teeth had been clenched through them were carried in to the hospitals. Without hesitation and in the most unpromising circumstances the doctors tackled the seemingly hopeless tasks with which they were confronted. In those places where there was no doctor within reach—and there were many— nurses performed tasks far beyond those for which they were trained. And in the many parts where even the services of nurses were not available, ordinary missionaries who had had training such as is given by the Missionary School of Medicine took their courage in their hands and carried on.

But the astounding fact is that with the 'broken dinner knives' which were the best in the way of equipment which these doctors could get, the percentage of cases lost was remarkably low.

Hospitals have been improved since those early days. As God supplied the means, better buildings were erected. Often the doctors themselves, in addition to their medical and surgical work, had to set and supervise the making of the bricks and the construction of the buildings. These original buildings have had wings added to them, until the earliest are hidden amid a host of supplementary rooms. But even in recent days, while something of the gleaming tiles and polished steel were in evidence, and electric light and X-Ray plants have come to the aid of the doctors, the visiting physician or surgeon from home could be forgiven if he were incredulous of the astounding work that was done under conditions which were so far below those which would be considered the barest minimum at home, or in Government hospitals anywhere.

Disease and death are terrifying to the heathen. Illness is thought to be caused either by an offended spirit or a curse. Nothing comes accidentally. It is the task of the witchdoctor to divine the reason for the sickness and to produce a remedy. The insanitary conditions in which the people live, their inadequate diet, and the floundering efforts of witchdoctors and others, combine to make the death-rate appallingly high.

When Protestant missions first commenced medical work in Congo it was with a view to meeting this condition. The need was overwhelming even when viewed solely from a humanitarian point of view; but when the background of unmitigated darkness, unrelieved by Gospel light, was taken into consideration, no words could describe its awfulness. Something had to be done. But how enormous the task! Malaria carried off its incredible quota. Sleeping sickness was rife. Elephantiasis, leprosy, yaws with the dysenteries and other intestinal infections together presented an alliance against which the efforts of the missions seemed trivial. What Government medical services existed were entirely inadequate. The Roman Catholics did little in this direction. Yet, called of God and separated unto the Gospel, doctors sacrificed their prospects in the homeland and went forth, 'the Lord working with them', and they performed wonders. Medical wonders. Surgical wonders. But through these and far beyond them in importance, spiritual wonders.

Great changes have, however, taken place since those days. The Belgian Government during its last few years in Congo made spectacular strides to regain the lost ground. Huge hospitals and dispensaries were built at a cost of many millions of francs. There were, however, insufficient European staff to man them.

Medical science has greatly reduced the incidence of the diseases which caused so much havoc in the early years. Sleeping sickness, which at one time carried off whole clans, was almost eliminated. Leprosy had reached the place where, for those who came in time and took the prolonged treatment, the disease could be arrested. Where it had produced deformity, it was being ameliorated by modern surgery. Even malaria, that old enemy of mankind in the tropics, was being steadily overcome. New drugs played their part in vanquishing these diseases, and war against the insect carriers helped. In Leopoldville, once a hotbed of malaria, the whole area was sprayed with insecticide from the air at frequent intervals, and the incidence of malaria fell unbelievably. In other towns, disinfection and spraying were carried out by teams of Africans.

New diseases have, however, found an entrance there as there has been more contact with the outside world. Venereal diseases, practically unknown at one time, have spread alarmingly; and tuberculosis has found in the African a victim with little resistance to its depredations. Cancer would appear to be more common. Allergies are coming to light, as well as vitamin-deficiency diseases.

While the Roman Catholics had little in the way of medical work on their own, they supplied a large part of the European nursing staff for the Government work. Many of the doctors and nurses, as well as the African staff, were active Catholics. The atmosphere in Government hospitals was distinctly Catholic, and pressure was brought to bear on patients to join that church.

In view of the changes which were taking place, the direction of Protestant medical work gradually changed. At first it was almost entirely a Gospel agency. As in the time of our Lord, the power of God shown in the healing of the sick was evidence of His power to save. Latterly, however, without losing any of its Gospel approach, it became more and more a ministry to the Protestant community. These people have emerged so recently from heathenism that the associated ideas which have been accepted for generations still find a response in their hearts. In times of illness, the pressure from heathen relatives and from weak Christians, combined with a residual regard for the old beliefs, form a very strong temptation to return to the witch-doctor and all that is associated with him. But the possibility of obtaining treatment under Christian auspices, surrounded by prayer and sympathetic and helpful ministry of the Word of God, make a strong appeal. Many are those whose faith has been rein-forced as in times of illness they have received loving and skilful help in our mission hospitals and dispensaries.

Approximately two hundred miles separated each of our four hospitals from its neighbour. In addition there were dispensaries on each of our twenty-one stations. There were leper camps in connection with ten of these. The over-busy doctors, in addition to the enormous clinics with which they had to deal, the operations they performed, and the maternity work, made periodical visits to these dispensaries and leper colonies. Considerably more than a million treatments were given annually, and over 1500 major operations performed. This is in addition to the care and treatment of about 8,000 leprous persons resident in the leper colonies. Needless to say, doctors and nurses were 'pressed out of measure, above strength', particularly since it must be borne in mind there are not all the modern facilities and labour-saving devices available on the mission field that are to be found at home.

Work on such a scale can only be done with the aid of African helpers. In addition to the overwhelming labours recounted above, the doctors found time to give two year courses of instruction to male and female assistant nurses. The help of these has proved invaluable. They were permitted to take charge of dispensaries and leper colonies where necessary, under occasional supervision by a doctor.

What of the spiritual results? Unless these are produced, the work is merely humanitarian. Not only have the African staff, as well as the Europeans, engaged in personal evangelism as they ministered to patients, but an African evangelist has been part of the regular personnel. His task has been to hold services for the patients, to visit the wards, and to take advantage of every opportunity of pointing the unsaved to Christ, or pleading with backsliders to return, of comforting the anxious and sorrowing, and to hold himself ready to give spiritual help whenever needed.

By these combined efforts, under the blessing of God, a steady stream of converts came forth. As in the homeland, so in Congo, and perhaps to a greater degree, hearts become tender in times of illness or anxiety and those who have hitherto been hardened to the pricks of conscience and the claims of God are made ready to listen and respond.

At Oicha, in the huge leper colony there, there is a church the entire membership (over 300) of which, together with its pastor and officers, is composed of those suffering from leprosy. Handicapped physically it is yet a healthy church spiritually. Its members give far more liberally than those of many other churches.

2. Wizards that peep and mutter

Witches, magicians and dealers in the occult of all ages and countries have much in common. With very little adaptation the stock-in-trade of Shakespeare's witches might be applied to the witchdoctors of Africa, who also display similarities to the Witch of Endor.

> Fillet of a fenny snake
> In the cauldron boil and bake;
> Eye of newt and toe of frog,
> Wool of bat and tongue of dog
> Adder's fork and blind-worm's sting,
> Lizard's leg and howlet's wing,
> For a farm of powerful trouble,
> Like a hell-throb boil and bubble.

Those who have examined the paraphernalia of an African witchdoctor will have seen similar articles.

Invariably one finds the tooth of leopard or lion, the claw of a bird, a horn filled with mysterious substances, and other strange things. One of his most important articles is a gourd with a stone in it which rattles. A forked stick with a whistle suspended from it is also inseparable from him.

Apart from the professional witchdoctors, there are people, usually women, who have a knowledge of herbal and other remedies which they use for treatment of disease and sometimes for more sinister purposes. There are also the rainmakers who sacrifice and perform certain rites in time of drought.

Much of the art of the witchdoctor consists of chicanery, sleight of hand and deception. Converted witchdoctors have often told us of their deception in supposedly extracting seeds, stones, or other objects from the bodies of the sick. One such practitioner professed to be able to discover a thief. When a robbery took place in the chief's village, all those who lived there were lined up, and the old man went slowly along the line with a gourd filled with water in his hand, muttering incantations. He paused over the outstretched hand of each. Nothing happened until he came to a certain poor defenceless old man; and then a stream of water came from the spout of the gourd on to the old fellow's hand. A missionary who was present asked to see the gourd. Examination revealed the fact that pressure applied or relaxed over a hole in the gourd controlled the flow of the water. He, therefore, lined the people up again, and when he came to the witchdoctor caused the water to spurt on his hands, and later showed all the people how it was done. The witchdoctor was thereupon chased from the village.

Yet there are many among the witchdoctors who

have contact with the spirit world, and who possess a 'familiar spirit'. A talk with one whom we had long known as a famous witchdoctor, and bitterly opposed to the Gospel, but who had subsequently come to Christ and renounced his infamous craft, revealed the undoubted fact that he had had a 'familiar spirit'. He could summon this spirit at will. By the aid of this spirit he was able to trace the whereabouts of stolen property. Sometimes he did this by the use of half a gourd filled with water, which was used much in the same way as the diviner's crystal. He described how on one occasion, among others, when he had been asked to find a hoe which had disappeared, the familiar spirit had led him by stages to a crevice in the rock in which lay the instrument in question.

Some times he was asked to find out who had been responsible for the death of a certain person. He would enter his dark hut alone, and by means of his gourd rattle he would summon the spirit of the departed. At his call a spirit would arise in the name of the dead and so impersonate him that his voice could be recognized by relatives outside the hut.

From time to time the witchdoctor was asked to visit a particular village in order that it might be protected from illness. On his arrival, everyone in the village stood. His first action was to pass his long forked stick round the bounds of the village to keep the illness away.

Then a sheep was killed. The witchdoctor would examine the carcass and remove the intestines. He then came to the people. Each male stood before him. He made each to revolve three times, then crouch and pass between his legs. If the man was unusually tall, he would have to revolve four times and then pass under his right arm. (One particular witchdoctor was very short, and people had the greatest difficulty in passing between his legs). The thought behind this symbolic action was that they were leaving sickness behind when they passed between the witchdoctor's legs, and entering into health.

The next part of the ceremony was that a small portion of a strange and secret medicine was placed in the nostril of each.

Then food was cooked—the millet meal was sprinkled in boiling water and stirred to make a thick dough, the staple diet of that part. Children brought large leaves, and a portion of the dough together with a piece of liver and meat was placed on it, and wrapped in it. A young child was then called and instructed to place the bundle on the path leading to the village. Similar offerings were placed on each of the paths in the vicinity. The idea behind this was that the spirits would eat and be satisfied before they came to the village, and so would not come and give illness to the villagers.

In return for such service, the witchdoctor was given a high fee. His was a lucrative practice.

On one occasion, immediately after the visit of the witchdoctor severe illness broke out in the village. Many women and children died, and one of the elders of the clan also passed away. There was great sadness and consternation, and the witchdoctor was discredited.

Came a time when in answer to many prayers the witchdoctor himself was converted. He made open confession of his misdeeds. Said he 'I have done much of Satan's work and have received nothing. Satan deceived me. I have consumed people's possessions, and have practised much guile and fraud. I am a wicked man. I must believe in Jesus. He died for me.'

He lived on in his village for a number of years, bearing bright testimony to the One in whom he had found life indeed, and deliverance from the evil bondage which had enchained him for so long.

This was by no means the only witchdoctor who was converted. Many of these servants of the evil one have, in answer to the prayers of the Lord's people and through their persistent testimony, been brought to the knowledge of Him who is mighty to save. Paraphernalia worth large sums has been brought into the open and burned in the presence of large crowds, and some who were enemies of the truth have become its advocates.

3. A TAILOR TURNED

Mishele was a tailor. Years ago he had obtained a sewing-machine and had started to make garments for sale. As he prospered he bought another machine and another, and employed boys to stitch the garments he cut out. Before long he was a wealthy man. He had been brought up as a Roman Catholic, and he was a staunch follower. The time came, however, when he was taken ill. He was taken to the local dispensary, and from thence to the hospital. But little help could be given him. He was told that he must rest as far as possible as his heart was in a very bad condition.

The tailor realised that this was a serious matter. He might die at any time. And the thought of death terrorised him. Was there nothing he could do? The reputation of a doctor some 400 miles north of where he lived had reached him. It would be an expensive journey to go there, but his condition was desperate, and he determined that, at any cost, he would make the trip. So taking advantage of a lorry which was going that way he went, taking his wife with him to look after him.

The only thing about this doctor which caused him some concern was that he was a Protestant, and his hospital was on a Protestant mission station. However, since he knew of this in advance, he felt that he could arm himself against anything which would draw him away from the Catholic faith.

Arriving at the hospital, and awaiting treatment, he was invited to go with the crowd of patients to the chapel service. But he immediately refused. Such things were not for him, a Catholic. He must shut his ears to the Protestant teaching.

Nevertheless, he could not help wondering what the Protestants taught. After all, if he knew, maybe he could correct some of the false ideas they had planted in the minds of others. He decided that while he could not attend the service, there was no harm in sitting at a distance and catching something of what was being said. But sitting at a distance was not too satisfactory. He could hear a few words, but not enough to get the gist of the address. So he found himself drawing nearer and nearer to the chapel in which the services were held. The windows were large and if he sat close enough he could hear the preacher.

One day in particular, the address was given by the hospital evangelist. The tailor was deeply moved by it. He told the evangelist later that as he listened, the word had laid hold of his whole body, even to his legs and arms, and his heart had burned within him.

'That', said the evangelist, 'is the Holy Spirit beginning to work within you.'

The following Sunday found him sitting in the large

station chapel. The beloved doctor was the preacher. After the conclusion of the service, Mishele was among those who stayed behind for counselling. Wise helpers led him to trust no longer in his good works or religious observances, but by simple faith to rest upon Christ.

The treatment for his condition was long. Many months he lived at the hospital. Before he returned to his own home he asked to be baptized. He was carefully examined, and the leaders were satisfied that he was a truly converted man through faith in the Saviour. When he was baptised, he took the name of Daniel. His wife is also a believer, but had not at that time been baptised.

When the day came for him to leave, he stood up and gave his testimony. He told how formerly he was filled with fear. He was afraid to die. In spite of the fact that he was a Roman Catholic, he consulted the witchdoctors because of his heart trouble; but he found no satisfaction. Now that he knew that Christ was his personal Saviour he had peace of heart he never knew before, and was filled with joy. He no longer feared death for he knew that it would usher him into the presence of his Saviour.

4. FREEDOM FOR THE CHIEF

Chief Zunguraka sat at his beerpots day after day. Sin and evil customs had enchained him, but he had no desire to be free. He preferred his sin. The Gospel messengers came again and again and told him of freedom from sin and from condemnation through a Saviour who had died and risen again. He listened politely, though stolidly; but he was quite unmoved.

Not so his wives, however. They listened intently whenever the evangelist or the missionary told of heaven and how one could go there. The first wife particularly was conscious of a desire to know more. She would have responded to the Saviour, but she felt that she was not free. She was bound to follow her husband, and therefore her desires went no further. Time and time again the good news was given to the chief; but his heart was hard. 'Whoredom and wine and new wine take away the heart' (Hos. 4. 11).

But God has His way of dealing with those whom He purposes to save. The Chief developed a swelling in his neck. It seemed of little importance, and nothing to worry about. But it increased and he began to be concerned about it. As usual he sent for the witch-doctor. He came with all his paraphernalia and followed the usual ritual, promising that the trouble would soon be over. But his prophecies were not fulfilled. The trouble grew steadily worse. Further consultation with the witchdoctor, and further sacrifices followed. More was paid in fees to the practitioner. But all his incantations and ceremonies were of no avail. The swelling continued to grow.

At last he decided that the only thing to do was to go to the hospital and see what the doctor could do. So with his three wives and his attendants and retinue he made his way to Oicha. He was received with kindness. The good doctor gave him a thorough examination with the help of his African assistants. At length the verdict was given—an operation would be necessary.

It was somewhat of a shock, but other patients came round and assured him that with the medicine the doctor gave which put them to sleep he would feel nothing. And when he awoke, the swelling would be gone. But did they all wake up again, he wondered.

Suppose he should be one of those who did not come to?

Then the hospital evangelist came along and presented the claims of Christ to him. The doctor and nurses did their part. He began to attend the chapel services and there he heard more of the love of God in Christ. At last came the day when the chief took the decisive step of receiving Christ as his Saviour and confessing him publicly.

He went to see the pastor of the church and told him how that ever since he had come to the hospital he had been conscious of the Holy Spirit working in his heart. At last he had come to Christ and was determined to follow Him fully. The first thing to be put right was his polygamy. He was determined to send his last two wives to their homes, and retain only the first. She has now put her confidence in the Saviour and has been baptised.

Says the hospital evangelist, 'Medical work is a trap which catches the people of the devil'.

5. THE WITCHDOCTOR DOCTORED

Everybody knew Matete. Everybody, that is, in the Monandi tribe. Was he not the clever witchdoctor? Was he not in contact with the spirits? Did he not know the mysteries of secret potions which could be given to enemies that they might die, or which could bring about desired results in other directions? No other witchdoctor like him! Many had gone to him for a solution of their problems. He had grown wealthy with the presents they had brought.

But he was an old man now, and he had his own problems. He had long-continued trouble in his intestines. Try as he would, nothing seemed able to cure it.

He had sacrificed repeatedly. He had sought the aid of the spirits; but nothing helped.

At long last he came to the conclusion that he would try the Protestant hospital. He had heard so much about it. Cases which had been too much for him had found speedy cure there. So he made his way through the forest road to the hospital. There were hundreds of people there. Many had come hundreds of miles to consult the doctor. Some had come in cars and lorries. The weekly bus always brought new patients for treatment. And there were Europeans too, not only missionaries but Greeks and Belgians and others.

He was given a place in which to stay. He had not been long in it when the faithful evangelist came to see him. After opening up conversation he pointed out to him that he needed more than physical help. He needed forgiveness and salvation. The doctor and his helpers might be able to provide the help that was required on the physical level; but his spiritual needs could only be met by accepting the Saviour. Patiently the evangelist told him of his danger, not only of death, but of the judgment which follows. He turned to the Scriptures and read to him the verse which says 'the fearful, the unbelieving, and the abominable, and murderers and whoremongers and sorcerers and idolators and all liars shall have their part in the lake which burneth with fire and brimstone; which is the second death.' Sorcerers! He was a sorcerer! All the paraphernalia of his art was there in his hut! But they had failed to help him, and because of them he was in eternal peril! But there was a way of escape. There was a Saviour who had taken the sinner's place and had died for him. He had only to turn to Him to find forgiveness, freedom and hope.

The finger of God touched the old man's heart and conscience. He trembled as he heard of these things. As he thought of what he had heard he felt he must learn more. He made his way to the house of the evangelist. There the seeker—poor, ignorant, sinful Matete—found the Saviour, or was found of Him. Matete confessed his evil ways and told of his determination to turn from them.

As soon as he was discharged from the hospital, he returned to his home. It was not long before he called for the local evangelist and told him what had taken place. Then, when the people had gathered together, he brought out the apparatus of his trade—claws of birds, lions' teeth, lizard and snake skins, horns full of secret medicines, and his forked staff—and burned them all.

He has since joined the catechism class and hopes to be baptised.

CHAPTER IV

FROM SLAVERY OF SIN TO FREEDOM OF SONSHIP

1. FARANKA MOKO

'THOSE who wish to receive Jesus Christ as their Saviour now, please raise their hands.'

A forest of hands was raised. Everyone did his best to respond. But what hands! Some were normal. But many had no fingers, some had fingers and arms that were deformed. Some had nothing but pads for hands. Some were hidden among the diseased bodies, for their owners had to sit on the floor.

The missionary felt sure that they had not understood. After all, the Gospel message was new to them. He had brought several Africans, some of whom he had taught to play the cornet, to assist him in holding an evangelistic service at the Government Leper Camp some sixty miles from the mission station at Banda. It was clear to the missionary that further simplification of the message was called for.

So he went over the ground again. All people had turned to their own way, away from God. Some had worshipped and served spirits in place of the true God. Some had lived wicked lives. None had loved and served God as they should. All had evil hearts inherited from Adam, and so they committed sin, and all were under condemnation. But God in His great love and mercy had sent His Son, who had taken the place of those who were guilty; had died for their sins;

AT THE COTTON MARKET

A CONGOLESE VILLAGER HANGS OUT MAIZE TO DRY

AFRICAN POLICEMAN DIRECTING TRAFFIC AT A BUSY CROSSROADS IN LEOPOLDVILLE

THE MONUMENT TO STANLEY AND OTHER PIONEERS OF CIVILIZATION AT LEOPOLDVILLE

and those who received Him as their own Saviour would be forgiven. This was an individual matter. As none could eat and so satisfy another's hunger, but each must eat for himself, so each must receive the Saviour for himself if he wished to be saved.

Again he made the appeal. The result was precisely the same. Each one did his best to raise his hand.

'Ah!' thought the missionary, 'surely the disease has affected their minds, and dulled their brains. They cannot fully grasp what I am trying to get across to them.'

So again he went carefully over the same ground, putting the Gospel message as simply as he could. Then he asked all to leave the building, and those who genuinely wished to open their hearts that the Lord Jesus might come in and cleanse them should re-enter.

Slowly and laboriously the congregation made its way out of the mud and wattle chapel. Few could walk normally. Some hobbled in the peculiar way which marks those who have fallen arches, or have sores on their feet. Many leant on sticks as they dragged their deformed limbs out of the building. Some, having lost the power of their legs, could only shuffle along the ground on their haunches. Others were blind and had to be led out.

At last the chapel was emptied. When the last one had left, the process was reversed, and the whole crowd came back again.

There was nothing to do but to interview each one personally. But this only brought out the fact that they understood perfectly what they were doing.

How did this come about? How had they been so prepared to respond to the claims of Christ?

Among the crowd was Faranka Moko. Why he had

4

been given such a name nobody knows. Literally 'One
Franc,' perhaps most nearly translated colloquially as
'Old Tuppenny.' He was a sorry figure. His hands
were simply pads, his fingers having dropped off long
ago. His feet had no toes. His eyes could no longer
see. He had lost the use of his legs, and had to shuffle
along the ground, propelled by his hands. Seemingly
useless, what could such an one do for the good of
others?

In his youth he had been a personal servant of the
great Chief Mapoi—the last chief to oppose the
Belgians. The chief often entrusted important missions
into his hands for he was bold and uncowed by the
white man, yet polite with it all. But when the chief
was finally defeated and driven across the river into
French territory, Faranka Moko remained behind, and
settled in his own home.

He was happily married. But before many years had
passed, the dread disease of leprosy showed itself. The
Africans of that part believe that it may be caused by
eating the flesh of the red bush pig. He probably
thought that an enemy had introduced a piece of such
flesh secretly into his food. Be that as it may, the disease
had got a hold of his body, and nothing that could be
done by way of sacrifice or offering, or by the witchdoctor had the power to remove it.

His wife stayed with him valiantly for a long time,
but as the disease gradually gained a stronger hold
over him, she felt she must leave him. Reluctantly she
went to her home, and was subsequently married to
another man.

Faranka Moko had heard the Gospel before. Some
years previous to the service recounted above, a new
mission station had been opened at a place called

Banda. Among the activities undertaken there, a refuge was opened for people suffering from leprosy. Treatment, which even then was more promising than anything which had been tried before, was commenced on about thirty-five lepers. Among them was Faranka Moko.

Needless to say, this little group not only received medicines, they were also told of God's love in the provision of a Saviour. But as far as could be seen at the time, no impression was made on Faranka Moko. That, however, was simply due to the dimness of human sight; for down in that dark heart there was the beginning of a response of which only God was aware.

As has so often happened, there were no missionaries available to maintain the station at Banda. When the pioneers who had opened it went on furlough, there was nothing for it but to close the work.

A Government leper colony was being started some distance away, and the little group of unfortunates was taken there. Treatment was given, houses and food were provided. But there was one big difference—there was nobody to tell them of God. Faranka Moko could not preach, but in conversation with others he told what he had heard at the mission station. And as he chatted around the fires, all the people in the camp became familiar with the Gospel message. Therefore it was that when the evangelist came and an appeal was made, all responded.

Faranka Moko responded too. It was the first open confession he had made of his faith in the Lord Jesus. But he avers that it was back at the mission station that he truly believed.

Not long after, the Government Leper Colony was closed. Faranka Moko returned to his village; but he longed to go back to the mission station—by now it had been reopened—and live there. One day the missionary came to the village in which he was living. Faranka Moko begged him to give him a lift in his car to the mission station; but unfortunately the missionary was going on a long journey in the opposite direction. However, he promised that one day when he was going that way he would help him. But months passed, and the missionary did not have occasion to come that way.

One day a deformed shape was seen shuffling its way into Banda station.

'Faranka Moko! But how did you manage to get here?'

'Friends carried me part way. I travelled the rest of the way on my haunches.' He had travelled about twenty-five miles propelling himself along the gravelled road with his fingerless hands.

The Banda Leper Colony had by now been re-opened. Faranka Moko soon took the place of leader and counsellor to the patients. He could never learn to read, but he gained a remarkable knowledge of the Scriptures. Were any in soul trouble? They went to him, and from his Spirit-given acquaintance with the Word he was able to lead them to the Saviour. To him also went believers faced with special problems or temptations, and he would give wise spiritual counsel.

He is an old man now. At first sight his appearance is repulsive. But his inward eyes are fixed on the heavens.

'It won't be long now,' he said when I saw him. 'I shall soon have the use of my legs again. Do you know what I am going to do then? I shall "walk and leap and praise God", like the man who was healed by

Peter and John. And I shall soon be able to see again. And when my eyes are opened, the first face I shall see will be that of Jesus!'

Praise God for such trophies of grace!

You who have full and joyful use of all your faculties, are they yielded to the Saviour for His use and Glory? This man, crippled, blind, and diseased, has handed all the little that there is left of him over to the Saviour, and He has greatly used him.

2. GOATS, GRASSHOPPERS AND GRACE

Goats! To the European living in Africa, anathema! They seem able to elude the care of any herder, and find their way into gardens. As to their tastes, they have no aversions. They will devour the young vegetables in a garden, or the flowers surrounding a house. They will ruin the maize crop of the African, or anything else in the fields. They have an insatiable appetite for paper, and unless school supplies in the little mud-and-wattle schools are well protected, they will 'inwardly digest' the books, but fail to 'read, mark or learn' the contents. Given the opportunity they will devour the clothes on the line, or the tea-towels drying on the table by the kitchen. They enjoy the gravelled motor roads, where they love to bask in the sunshine, or try to cross to the other side of the road just as the car is passing. They are one of the chief nuisances of Africa.

But this is simply the European point of view. To the African they are wealth. With them he buys his wives, wives for his sons and dependants. With them he pays the fees of the witch doctors, and they are also used for sacrifice and for divination. In time of need they can be turned into hard cash with which to clothe or feed the owner and his family, or pay their fines when they fall foul of the law. And from time to time they form the 'pièce de résistance' at a feast.

One thing, however, is agreed upon—both by blacks and whites—goats must be looked after, especially during the wet season when the young crops are growing.

And so it came about that on a certain occasion, out of occasions innumerable, two young lads were herding the goats and cows belonging to their father. They had left the village in the morning and were spending the day on the steep hillsides between Kasengu and Ara overlooking Lake Albert. And their mother had given them a snack to stave off the pangs of hunger until they returned to the village in the evening. She had wrapped it up in a broad banana leaf. It consisted of fried grasshoppers!

Fried grasshoppers! The very mention of the word is enough to make the African's mouth water. These grasshoppers belong to the locust family. The ordinary desert locust which appears in swarms is about four inches long, and brown. These grasshoppers are exactly the same in shape and appearance, but they are bright green in colour. They make their appearance during the night. When they appear, the news is sounded out over the countryside and shrill calls rend the air. All the world and his wife rise and go out into the darkness with flaming torches to gather them. The missionary hears the sound and turns in his bed. He knows well that the next morning the school children and all the people will be heavy with sleep, for the grasshoppers have appeared. When caught, the grasshoppers are impaled on reeds or straws, taken home and fried. They are regarded as a very great delicacy by the Africans, and some missionaries relish them too, but not all.

At midday, or earlier, following the habit of boys the world over, the two lads sat down to enjoy the tasty snack which their mother had given them. They unwrapped the banana leaves, and there were the greasy, crisp grasshoppers. This was luxury indeed!

Dengi was the elder of the two. He was a quiet, meditative boy, and his thoughts were long and deep. For some time a serious question had been troubling his mind. It came to the surface as they ate and chatted. The day was long. The sun was hot. There was no need to hurry, and they sat leisurely and chatted away as they enjoyed the rich repast.

At length Dengi came out with a question for his brother:

'With whom would you be prepared to share your grasshoppers?'

That was a big question, and his brother hesitated somewhat before replying.

'I don't know. I suppose if I had a wife I would share them with her,' he said. 'Who would you share yours with?'

Dengi answered slowly and thoughtfully.

'If I knew who had created me, I would share my grasshoppers with my Creator.'

Thus the question which had lain at the back of his mind so long and which had troubled him by day and night found expression. But nobody could give him the answer. He asked in vain. Many moons must yet pass before he could find any answer to the queries aroused in him by the Spirit of God. But God had implanted the question and He would give the answer to it at the right time.

What was that? . . . The whole village stopped their work as they heard the faint rhythmic sound of a distant drum. The men stopped their hoeing in the garden. The women paused as they searched for firewood or drew water from the spring.

The chief called the people to come to work in his garden by means of a drum; but this was not from that direction. Drums were beaten at dances; but this was not a dance rhythm. Nor was it a drum for mourning. Yet each morning the sound came over the hills and valleys. The men talked about it. So did the women. Even the children listened for it each morning. It was the subject of conversation as the people sat round their fires in the evening.

Before long one of the elder men discovered the answer, and passed it on to the others:

'It is sounded by a man who has come to live in a village away over the hills to tell about the God who created all things. He sounds the drum to call people to go to hear about their Creator.'

Dengi's heart leapt within him. Was this the answer to the question which had troubled him so long? How he would love to go to hear what this man had to teach. But his father would never hear of him leaving the goats and taking such a trip.

The early missionaries of the Africa Inland Mission had made their way over from Kenya, and armed with a somewhat grudging permission obtained from the authorities, through the intervention of President Theodore Roosevelt when he came on his hunting trip to Africa, had crossed Lake Albert and had climbed the steep slopes on the western side of the Lake, and after some delays had settled at Kasengu and later at Ara. There they had set to work to learn the Alur language and to translate portions of the Scriptures into that tongue, while at the same time they told to all those within their reach that God, the Creator of all things, loved them as He loved all the world, and had sent His Son to die for their sins. The emancipating message forced its way into the understanding of some of the dark skinned Alurs of that part, and the time came when some of them took the great step of faith by which they became linked with the Saviour. What a change this involved in their lives and outlooks. They were saved! No longer could the old satisfy! The new loyalty demanded that they break with the past evil practices and live 'unto Him who died for them and rose again'. Life became new as they experienced a new-found joy, and a peace of heart of which they had known nothing before. Trials, opposition and suffering were often involved; but they came through and went on to know more of Him who had loved them and had given Himself for them. They learned to read, and after a few plodding months could understand something of the Scripture portions distributed among them.

But this news was too good to be kept to themselves. Was it true that those who believed not were bound for eternal misery? Then they must warn them, and give them the good news of a way of salvation. So, separated by the Holy Ghost, they went out to different parts of the tribe. It was one of such who had gone to the hills near Dengi's village, had erected a mud hut for himself and sounded the drum daily to call the people to hear the Word of God.

Only a short time after Dengi had heard about the evangelist, his desires to hear more were stronger than he could endure. One day, as he was herding the goats, he felt that he could wait no longer. So leaving the cattle in the care of his brother, he ran away over the hills to find the place from which the sound of the drum emanated. There he went to lodge with the evangelist. He heard not only of the One who had created him, but Who had also redeemed him, giving His own Son as a ransom. Led by the Spirit who had awakened the curiosity in the mind of this heathen lad, Dengi stretched out the hand of faith and, in his simple way, received the Saviour as his own, and was born again.

Eager to learn more, he applied himself to the lessons given by the evangelist, and before long was able to spell out the words of Scripture in the booklets printed by the Scripture Gift Mission. He attended the catechism classes, and in due time was adjudged fit to be baptised.

It was a great occasion. They went down the steep hillsides to the river below. There the missionary immersed him and others as they made open profession of their faith, and of the accompanying facts of their death with Christ to the old life, and their resurrection in Him to walk in newness of life. He could never forget the occasion. Later they went to the mud chapel, and there he was received into the membership of the church.

Years have passed since then. Dengi has found a Christian wife and is the father of a family. He has his own compound, similar to that of many other Alurs. But there is no spirit-hut there. Nor is there the brewing of beer, nor can the broad leaves of the tobacco plant be seen. But from that centre he bears consistent testimony to the One who has saved him, and is a staunch, well-established member of the local church. He is typical of many others in that tribe.

3. THE RETURN OF DAWIDI KAVEVE

'Go and tell Dawidi to put away those things which prevent him preaching My Word and which deceive others also. Go at once.'

In the early days of the Africa Inland Mission in Congo, three single ladies occupied a site at Ara on the hills overlooking Lake Albert. One of these was Miss Sarah Stirton. Among those she employed to help her in various tasks was a little lad called Kaveve. He waited on her in the house, and won his way to her heart. Miss Stirton gave a great deal of time to the translation of the Scriptures into the Alur language, and Kaveve was her chief advisor. Under her instruction he learnt of the Saviour and came to trust Him. When he was baptised he adopted the name of Dawidi (David). As he assisted in the translation of the New Testament he gained a knowledge of English which he was eventually able to speak fluently. He married a fine Christian girl.

Africans are far from being the only people who cannot stand up under prominence and importance. Dawidi's ego swelled as he realised the dependence which was placed upon him. He became self-assertive and over important, and eventually impudent. Miss Stirton had to call in the aid of a senior missionary in order to make him leave the station where he had become so objectionable.

But Miss Stirton did not fail to pray for him, and enlisted the prayers of many on his behalf. It was with great sadness, however, when she heard that he had taken a second wife, and at the same time had fallen into the devil's trap in other ways and began drinking and smoking hemp. He knew better, however, and, in an attempt to quieten the accusations of his conscience, he dismissed his second wife about six years later. But the other habits he had acquired were too strong for him, and he continued in them. He obtained work under the Government and was soon receiving a high salary. After serving for many years he was pensioned, and returned to his home with his first wife, who had remained true to him and to the Lord throughout all her husband's wanderings.

In the year 1957, a relative of Dawidi's lay dying. He realised that he had not long to live. He thought of death and the future with fear. 'It is appointed unto man once to die, and after death the judgment.' He knew something of the Gospel, but had never become a partaker of it. As he dwelt on these things, he felt he must do something, and that quickly, if he were to be assured of a bright eternity. Where could he get help? His mind turned to his relative Dawidi who, although he had backslidden, had never entirely given up his profession of Christianity. So he called for him, and when he arrived told him of his need for help in the things of God. Dawidi, from his own experience, from his knowledge of the Scriptures, and from what he had remembered of the lessons learnt many years ago on the mission station, was able to point him to the Saviour. When he left he had the satisfaction of knowing that his relative had taken the step of receiving the Saviour. The man later died in faith.

Shortly afterwards a woman relative had a dream. She saw a huge lorry filled with people in white clothing. Among them she recognised the dead relative. In the middle of the people, and wearing glistening garments was One whom she knew was the Son of God. As she watched that central figure, he turned to her, and pointing at her with his outstretched arm, spoke the words recorded at the beginning of this chapter. The command was urgent. She arose in the night and made her way over the hills to Dawidi's village. The dawn was breaking as she arrived. He was not yet up. She went to his hut and called for him. When he emerged she gave him the message with which she had been entrusted.

Dawidi was greatly impressed. Without hesitation he entered his hut and appeared again bringing with him his beerpots. He emptied the remainder of the brew on the ground, broke the earthenware pots into a thousand pieces and stamped on them. He brought out his pipes, made of gourds, and broke them. The remains of the hemp he threw on the fire in the view of all the neighbours. The next Sunday he attended the church service and asked to be permitted to say a few words. He made full confession of his misdeeds, and asked for forgiveness and the prayers of the Lord's people.

We were travelling over that hilly country organizing churches and instructing the believers and their officers. As we mingled with the crowd, I heard some fellow-missionaries holding a conversation with an African in English. I turned, and saw the smiling face of Dawidi Kaveve. He is now full of the joy of the Lord, and has been fully restored. He is now a deacon and the treasurer of the local church. His enthusiasm and knowledge of the Word are of tremendous help to the work of God.

4. Siku Moya

Dark are the depths of the Ituri forest, and dark are the practices followed there. 'The things which the

Gentiles sacrifice, they sacrifice to demons and not to God.' And the elder of the clan whose business it was to officiate at the sacrifices was the father of Siku Moya. Many were the goats he slaughtered in offering to the spirits. But he died when still comparatively young. Siku Moya, being the firstborn, was the one to take his father's place in leading the approaches to the spirits. He, however, was still a lad.

A stranger came to live in their village. He was alone, and unmarried. He therefore had nobody to cook for him, or to help in the work of the garden. Following the custom of the tribe, Siku Moya's mother sent portions of food to the stranger from time to time, observing how poor and lonely he was. One evening in particular, when she had prepared the evening meal for the family, she called her son to her.

'Take this to the stranger', said she. 'Go to his hut, say "Hodi", wait for him to reply "Karibu", and then give him the food.'

Siku Moya picked up the bowl of food, and made his way to the stranger's hut. The door was closed. He was about to knock at the door and say 'Hodi!' as he had been instructed, when he heard a voice inside, and realised that the stranger was speaking to somebody. Politely he waited. But the voice continued speaking, so at length the lad tapped on the door, and gave the call. Immediately the stranger replied 'Karibu!' Siku Moya opened the door and, on the invitation of the stranger, entered the hut. He looked round the hut searching for the visitor to whom the stranger had been speaking. But he could see nobody. He was apparently alone in the hut.

'Who were you talking to when I came? I heard you speaking to somebody,' asked Siku Moya.

'I was talking to my Father in heaven,' replied the stranger.

'Does He hear?'

'Yes, He always hears when His children speak to Him, and He answers their prayers.'

This was something quite new to Siku Moya. During the months that followed, he was always ready to take a dainty dish of food to the stranger, and to learn from him more and more of the Father in heaven.

Some time later the order came for everybody to be vaccinated. This was an innovation for the people there. Why should they be treated in this way? To protect them from smallpox, did they say? But did the white people not know that the disease was caused by offended spirits, or by poison given by someone with a grudge, or by a curse or the evil eye? How could the disease be cured without consulting the spirits, or sacrificing? Some said that it was a device of the white man to do them harm.

So the gossip went among the people. They all became agitated and decided to run away and hide in the forest. When the Government doctor arrived with his team, none were to be found.

An angry scene ensued. The official sent for the local headman, and asked why the people were not there. The headman made some excuse to cover himself. The official demanded that they should be searched for immediately, arrested, and sent to him for punishment.

The cringing headman saluted and went off with a few local police to where the people were hiding in the forest. Before long a line of prisoners tied together with ropes round their necks made their dejected way to the official's office. Siku Moya was among them. It was his first experience of imprisonment and he was terrified.

As he was being led away, his mother saw him and came close to him.

'My son,' said she, 'you remember that large pot of beer I am making and which is now brewing—I am going to offer it to the evil spirit that he may cause you to be released. Pray earnestly to him and beseech him to work for you.'

Long and earnestly did Siku Moya pray as his mother had bidden him that he might be released. But there was none that answered. He spent his first night in prison.

When the next morning dawned, the prisoners were set to weed the lawn in front of the Government office. Siku Moya was placed on his own at some distance from the others. As he worked there came to his mind again and again the memory of the stranger in his village whose God heard and answered prayer. At length his thoughts crystallised into resolution. He would pray to the Stranger's God. He bowed his head and expressed himself simply.

'God of the strange teacher! If you are God, cause me to be released, and You shall always be my God.'

Shortly after he saw two of the guards coming in his direction. They had been sent to set him at liberty.

He raced back to the forest thinking but one thought: 'The God of the strange teacher is my God!'

His mother was overjoyed to see him.

'See, my son, the evil spirit has heard our prayers. He shall have that pot of beer I promised.'

Siku Moya was but a lad. Nevertheless he refused to acknowledge the evil spirit, or to make offering to him. 'It was the God of the stranger Who heard my

A MODERN CONGOLESE HOME

CONGOLESE BUILDERS CONSTRUCTING A HOUSE

TWO LEADING
CONGO PASTORS

A PYGMY IN CONVERSATION
WITH A CONGOLESE OF
ANOTHER TRIBE

prayer, and not the evil spirit.   I will worship Him.'

The years have rolled by since that day. Siku Moya maintained the position he had taken. He attended the local chapel and learned all he could of his newly-found God. He put his trust in Jesus Christ. Attending school, he learned to read and studied the Word of God for himself. Later he was baptised and admitted to membership of the church.

His attitude changed towards the white man's medicine. And later he asked to be trained as a medical assistant at Oicha.

5. CAN A DEAD MAN SAVE OTHERS?

'Mahomet died many years ago. People go every year to visit his tomb at Mecca. How can a dead man save?'

The question posed itself in the mind of a Mohammedan woman who came over from Uganda for treatment. Not that she had been interested in the Gospel. Her heart was adamant against it when she arrived. Her father was a Pakistani, her mother an African woman from Toro in Uganda, and together they had prejudiced her mind against Christianity. 'Christianity,' said they, 'is the white man's religion. Mohammedanism is the religion of the coloured man.'

She came to the hospital simply and solely to get physical help. She had no desire or intention of listening to the message preached. She had to have surgical treatment, and that necessitated her staying at the hospital for a long time. The doctor, the missionary nurses, and the African assistants attended to her.

'How kind these people are!' she remarked to herself. Of course they were paid for their work, but they were so ready and willing to help. And they were so cheery! She had never seen anything like it. They did not put their own interests first, as did all the other people she had known!

And so when very gently they began to tell her about the One who was the secret of all their loving unselfishness, she was ready to listen, even though outwardly still opposed to the Gospel.

How gently and wonderfully does God work. So often it is not in the hurricane, the earthquake, or the fire, but in 'a voice of gentle stillness.' The Holy Spirit was speaking to that darkened soul in all the delicacy of His operations.

'Mohamet is dead. But Jesus Christ rose from the dead! He is alive. Therefore He can save!' Gently the thought impressed itself upon her.

But she was not yet ready to break with the past and to take any decisive step. She remained at the hospital for many months, recovering from her operation, and having treatment for the diabetes which had been discovered. When, at long last, the time came for her to leave and to return to her home in Uganda, she confided to the doctor that she had realised the efficacy of the death of Christ and had put her trust in Him. She asked for prayer.

It may be that there was at that time a slender strand of faith connecting her to the world's Saviour; but the work was far from complete. But He who begins a good work carries it on to the end. The God of all grace guided her footsteps. He would not quench the smoking flax, but tenderly watched over it. It was not by chance that back in Uganda she was brought face to face with the claims of Christ once more. Then she was ready to respond more wholeheartedly. 'Love so amazing, so divine' should have her all! Off came the charms and amulets to which she had clung. The sins which had marred her way were abandoned, and joyfully she stepped forth into the new life of freedom in Christ Jesus!

Tragedy had marked the old life. Her first husband had died. Soon after her second marriage her new husband took to drink, and gradually dragged her into it also. The inevitable consequence followed—they quarrelled and fought constantly.

Now life was different for her. But the tremendous change in her only emphasized the incompatibility of the union. After a while she came to the conclusion that it was impossible to live with the man and retain faith in the Redeemer. She therefore left him. She came to live at Oicha where the hospital is.

This 'brand plucked from the burning' was quite illiterate, but she set to work to learn to read. It took a long time before she could read the Book for herself.

There are many who make their way from Uganda for treatment at Oicha. They do not understand the languages of Congo, and so they cannot hear the Gospel as it is preached. Maria, as she is now called, built a little mud and wattle chapel from her own pocket, and there she conducts services in the Toro language. Her zeal is unbounded. When she is not preaching in that chapel, she is out and about among the many patients undergoing treatment, telling them of One who died for sinners, but Who rose again. Many have found forgiveness and liberty through her instrumentality.

6. THE QUESTION WHICH PERSISTED

Even African lads, happy as they may seem to be on casual acquaintance, have burdens. Yobu had his

many years before Independence brought its load of
perplexities for Congolese.

It weighed on his mind. He turned it over and over
in his thoughts as he herded his father's cattle by day.
It clamoured for an answer as he tossed on his hard bed
at night.

'Who made me? Who made all these things around
me?'

In vain he sought an answer from his friends.

His father, tall straight six feet of warrior as he was,
could give no help. 'Who knows?' was all he could
say by way of reply.

'Maybe the spirits' was the unsatisfactory answer he
got when he asked the elders of the clan.

And so the question continued to puzzle him.

The years passed by.

'Greetings to you.'

'Many greetings,' was the reply.

The wearied stranger had made his way along the
winding footpath, skirting rocks and thornbushes, and
had reached the place where Yobu was guarding the
herd.

That the stranger was a traveller was obvious, for
over his shoulder was hung a goatskin bag for his food,
and on his head was a rolled grass mat in which was
his blanket.

'Where have you come from?' The question might
imply an unwarranted inquisitiveness in European
circles; but there it merely indicated a polite
friendliness.

'I have come from Aba.'

'From Aba!'—for that meant a walk of eighty-five
miles, largely through the territory of a strange and
unfriendly tribe, and few made such a journey in those

days. Stories were rife of travellers who had been badly handled, and of some who had disappeared.

Yes, he had been to Aba where there was a Government centre, shops and a mission station. A relative had fallen ill there, and he had gone to visit him. The mission doctor had treated him very kindly, and had given medicine which had proved stronger than all the evil agencies which were supposed to have caused the disease.

There were houses there made of brick in which white people lived. Moreover the missionaries had shown them pictures, and told them of God who created all things.

Yobu started.

'God Who created all things!!!'

That was the very thing he longed to know. Here was the answer to the question which had persisted through the years. If only he could go to Aba and hear about that One. But even as he breathed the desire, he knew that it was impossible, unthinkable. His father would never agree to his taking that long, long journey, with all its nameless perils. So he had to be content with that clue to the answer to his problem.

The next link in the chain came some time later when he was sitting by the village fire. The village was simply a collection of mud huts with their thatched roofs and a few granaries, the whole surrounded by a palisade of poles the entrance to which could be closed at night.

A string of people came by.

Again the polite enquiry, 'Where have you come from?'

'We have been to the Chief's village.'

'What news?'

'A man is there who is telling the people about God who created all things.'

'Is he still there?' asked Yobu, intensely interested. 'Can I go and find him?'

'No, he has left. He said he would return in seven day's time and tell more.'

A mission station had been opened in the tribe, and an evangelist was going to the chief's compound each Sunday to preach the Gospel.

At long last, Yobu was in sight of the end of his questionings. Never had he found the days so long or so tedious as during that week. Not even during the long days when he herded the goats did the time drag with such leaden feet. Nevertheless the seven days at length came to an end, and at the earliest moment he set off with his brothers for the chief's compound.

There they listened as the evangelist told the amazing story of God who not only had created man and all things, but had done much more than that. Man had turned from God and had worshipped spirits, making offerings to them instead of to God. Moreover, in turning from God, man had sinned in many directions. Yet God loved man, while hating his sin, and had sent His Son to die in order that men might be forgiven.

When, at the close, the evangelist invited those who wished to receive the Son of God as Saviour to stand, all the family did so. They may not have fully understood, but their response indicated a desire in the right direction. For Yobu, however, it was decisive and irrevocable. From henceforth, he would follow Christ.

It was not long before he had to make a definite stand in his home. According to age-long custom, the first portion of food which each broke off as he dug into the heap of solid dough, the *pièce de résistance* of the evening meal, was to be thrown to the ground as an offering to the spirits, and a portion was placed in the spirit hut which formed a part of every compound that they might be placated and look favourably on the family. But Yobu felt that he could no longer render this homage to the spirits now that he had turned to God. So, with a good deal of inward trepidation, he refused.

It was unbelievable. All the eyes of the family were turned on him. Such a thing was unheard of. How dare he? His father, seething with anger, turned to him, asking him if he wanted the clan to be visited with disease, or death, or famine? His foolishness might mean the extinction of them all. He must give the spirits the attention they had always had, and must have. These ideas might be all right for the white people, but for them, they dare not neglect the spirits. His mother joined in too. His brothers, although they had made their profession of conversion, were not prepared to stand by him in this.

So the young man had to stand alone. Yet not alone, for his new-found Saviour had promised never to leave him, but to stand by him through thick and thin. The arms of his hands were made strong by the hands of the mighty God of Jacob.

But the struggle was not finished. As often as they sat down to eat together, the argument was renewed. But nothing moved him.

When his brother was taken seriously ill, the blame fell on him. Was not this the proof of what they had said? Nobody could neglect the spirits with impunity. His foolhardiness and obstinacy were going to bring disaster to them all. They would call the witchdoctor, and he must take part in whatever sacrifice was demanded. There was nothing else for it.

But still he refused, and their anger against him was white-hot. He prayed; but there seemed to be no answer, and the disease strengthened its hold upon his brother's body.

At last a new idea came to him. He would take his brother to the mission station, and ask the missionary to treat him. While somewhat emaciated by the sickness, his brother was still heavy, and if he were to be carried to the mission, the help of several would be needed. But none dared to help. So Yobu, with the consent of the sick man whose feeble faith revived under the encouragement given by his older brother, took the invalid on his back, and staggered with him the weary miles which separated them from the mission station. Along the dusty footpaths he went with his load, skirting rocks and thornbushes, down into the valleys, crossing the river by its uncertain and breath-taking wooden bridge, up the steady climb on the other side until, at last, exhausted and weary he laid the sick man at the feet of the Bwana. With prayer and care, and the application of precious knowledge gained at the Missionary School of Medicine, the illness gradually subsided, and in due course the patient was able to return to his village.

But the opposition at home was more than Yobu could endure. It was not long before he returned to the station to tell the Bwana of his difficulties and to ask whether he could be given a job as a workman on the station so that he could live there and at the same time learn more of the things of God. Permission was gladly granted.

He attended the daily prayers and all the meetings,

eagerly drinking in the truths in the Word of God. But he could not be persuaded to attend the daily class at which reading was taught.

That was not for him. He would never be able to master that mysterious art. It was all right for children, but he was no longer a child. It was beyond him.

In the end, however, the Madame cajoled him into attempting it. She would give him special instruction on his own, and then, if he prayed, God would help him so that he could read the Scriptures for himself.

He came. It was a great step forward when he grasped the idea that the strange signs each represented a sound. Slowly he mastered the vowels.

But as for writing them on the slate, that was entirely out of his reach. His hard and horny hands refused to form the letters. But the Madame, carefully and patiently, took hold of the fingers and guided them in the formation of the weird signs.

He began to gain hope that maybe, after all, he would be able to read. The next hurdle was a difficult one, however. It was a long time before he could grasp that these letters could be joined together to make syllables. And then that syllables connected could make familiar words.

When she had progressed thus far, however, it was not long before he obtained a Scripture Gift Mission booklet, *The Way of Salvation*, and very slowly and hesitatingly, not without many a mistake, he began to read.

He read aloud, of course. And as he did so, others gathered around to listen as he made the book speak words. He read out wonderful words of Scripture, and people marvelled.

Sometimes, when he paused, they would ask questions. 'What did that mean?' He did his best to explain with the knowledge he had gained at the meetings. Before long he found himself preaching, giving out the Gospel message, and his heart warmed to it.

When the New Testament was published, he availed himself of it speedily.

Came the time when he was to be baptised. He was carefully examined. When did he first trust Christ? What had Christ done for him? How could the death of Christ on the Cross save him? What is Christ doing now? To these and many other questions, Yobu was able to give satisfactory answers, and to quote the chapter and verse for his replies. Evidence was also given of his changed life, and his walk worthy of the Gospel. With a full heart, the Bwana had no hesitation in baptising him with a multitude of others. As is usual in Africa, he took a new name from the Bible when he was baptised—Yakobo (Jacob).

Interest in the Gospel message was spreading. There were little groups of interested people in all parts of the tribe. Where there were sufficient, they got together, erected a little mud and pole chapel, and a hut for an evangelist, and asked that someone might be appointed to minister to them. Many young converts went out in response to these appeals, and out of their limited knowledge made the Saviour known.

There was one place at the extreme end of the tribe which was hard. No appeal for a preacher came from there. The people were satisfied with their heathenism, and teachers of another confession had prejudiced them against the Protestants. To that place, Yobu (or Jacob he must now be called) felt drawn. He went there. But oh! the persecution he met. They argued with him. They ordered him away. They threatened him. They tried to starve him, and to prevent food reaching him. He was beaten. He was manhandled. On one occasion he was set upon, and assailed till his enemies left him believing that he was nearly dead. But none of these things moved him. He continued through evil report and good report, in season and out of season, preaching the Gospel. And eventually there gathered around him a band of men and women whose hearts God had touched.

He is an old man now. His lack of education has prohibited him from entering even the lowest school for the training of evangelists. But he has absorbed the Word for himself, and has gone on faithfully preaching its message throughout the many years since he first heard. Broken in body by tropical diseases, but still undaunted in spirit, the trumpets of the other side may sound tumultuously at any time when he enters the eternal city.

7. PAGAN TO PASTOR

'That is not the path, Bwana. This is the one!' The stocky figure of the headman ran after the missionary who had taken the wrong fork of the path as he left the village.

The missionary had travelled far, tramping over the hills and down into the valleys searching for a suitable place to start a centre for evangelism. The afternoon was wearing on as he drew near to the village of the local headman. He heard a good deal of noise and excitement, and long experience told him that the men were carousing over the beerpots. This would be no time to hold a Gospel service.

He passed through the village, greeting the crowd as he went on his way. For days the women had been preparing the pots of strong drink. All the men of the district gathered and drank plentifully of it, their raucous laughter telling of the effects of the drinking. So preoccupied had they been with their excitement and mirth that they failed to hear the approach of the white man. Only when he passed and greeted them was there a moment of silence. They watched him as he went through the village with the men who accompanied him.

There were, however, several footpaths leading out of the village and the travellers took the wrong one. It only led to the spring where the women went to draw the water. The mistake was allowed of God!

It was the headman himself who noticed the error and ran after the missionary to show him the right path. Noting how strongly he smelt of drink, the missionary said, 'how can I know that you are directing me aright? You have drunk so much that you cannot think straight. You need somebody to show you the path to heaven. You need a Saviour!'

The headman was interested, and asked the white man who he was. He replied that he was a Protestant missionary, and was looking for a place for a chapel and an evangelist.

'Put it here!' said the headman. 'This is the place!'

'No,' said the missionary, 'you would not want the Gospel. If an evangelist were here he would tell you to turn to Christ, and that would mean giving up your drinking and wickedness. You would not want the Gospel here.'

But the headman insisted that they would be willing to give it all up if only he would send them a teacher.

How little we know of the results of apparently casual conversation. Seeds sown at random sometimes bear surprising harvest. Unknown to the missionary, the conversation led to the conversion of the headman. Before long a mud and wattle chapel was erected there, and eventually an evangelist arrived.

The headman was overjoyed. He attended the services, and did all he could to encourage the young people to join the classes which were commenced to teach them to read.

The first three to enrol were brothers, and for one of them, at least, God had great plans.

Their parents were witchdoctors, both the man and his wife. This brought them no small gain. They possessed large numbers of goats and fowls. Together they worked, and the results of their labours could be seen in large gardens which they cultivated. But in spite of all the artifices which they employed, they were often hungry, for as often as they planted their crops and they had sprung up with all the promise of an abundant harvest, they were invaded and destroyed either by wild pigs, elephants or monkeys.

Ten children were born to them, but in spite of all their sacrifices and professed occult powers, only four survived. The eighth child was a boy called Mwaka. When he was old enough, it became his duty to herd the goats and to take his part in watching the gardens to give warning of the approach of invaders from the forest.

So persistent were the wild animals in destroying their crops that later on the father, after consulting the spirits and carrying out the ceremonies of divination, decided that they should move. So another site was chosen, some miles from the former one.

The father only lived about a year after moving to the new place, and Mwaka was left to help his mother as best he could in the gardens, while his younger brothers herded the goats.

So they might have lived and died as many other heathen people do. But the living God had made eternal plans regarding Mwaka and the other members of that family. The mistaken path was the hinge on which swung the gate into those purposes.

That there is an enemy of all that is good, Satan who seeks to frustrate the plans of God, is nowhere more evident than on the mission field. Those who invade the domain where he has held undisputed sway throughout the centuries are soon made aware of his presence. And God's purposes regarding Mwaka were not to be allowed to go forward unchallenged. The evangelist who had been sent to the village had not long been converted. Sent out to stand alone in heathen surroundings, he was a ready prey to the devil's wiles. He stood for three weeks only. Then, falling into sin with one of the local girls, he left his post and ran across the border into Uganda. There was nobody else to fill the vacancy.

It was a sad blow to the three brothers, whose appetites had been whetted with a desire to go on. Poor Mwaka was disappointed and discouraged. He also ran across the border, and made his home with relatives in Uganda.

But God's hand is not stayed by international boundaries, and Mwaka could not excape it. He had no peace of heart there in Uganda because of the ardent desire which had been awakened within him to read the Word of God. He must and would learn, somehow or other.

So at the end of six months he returned to his home. There was still no evangelist to replace the one who had fallen. He heard of one at a more distant village, however. But it was too far off for them to attend daily school, but Mwaka and his brothers walked down the steep ravines and up again the other side every Sunday in order that they might hear the good news which was preached.

Mwaka bought a First Primer. He had already learned the meaning of some of the characters. So whenever a boy who had attended the classes came through the village, Mwaka stopped him and would not let him proceed until he had taught him something more from his First Primer. In this way he mastered the whole of the booklet, and also taught it to his two younger brothers.

He was not satisfied, however, but longed to read the Word of God. So he decided to take the long and arduous journey to the mission station to buy a Gospel of John. It was a long and trying day's walk. Mwaka had no money, but he took a chicken with him, which he would sell and so be able to purchase the book.

But when he arrived at the mission station, full of excitement at the prospect of procuring the book, he discovered that the missionary and his wife were away on a journey, and the bookshop was closed. The blow was too great, and he sat down as great hot tears made their way down his cheeks. He waited for four days, but there was no sign of the missionaries and, disappointed, he made his way back to his home.

There he continued to help his brothers to read the First Primer, and he enlisted others for his class also. Before long there was a little group of those who had mastered the first steps of reading.

By this time an evangelist had come to a village about four miles away. On one of his trips to the mission station he bought the Gospel of John so longed for by Mwaka, who was overjoyed to receive it.

When the missionary heard of the enthusiasm in Mwaka's home, he sent an evangelist there once again. He had only been there two weeks, preaching to the people the Gospel of salvation through the Lord Jesus Christ, when he asked who wished to believe in the Saviour. Mwaka made the great decision that day, and responded to the working of the Holy Spirit who had been leading and dealing with him.

The evangelist asked Mwaka if he would help him to teach. This he was glad to do, and whenever school was held, he was in his place doing his work. Occasionally, when the evangelist was called to the mission station, Mwaka preached the Word to those who came to the school. They were a mixed crowd. School in those days was not just for children. Older men and women, as well as others of all ages with a desire to be able to read the Bible for themselves, came to the little mud edifice where they struggled to master the significance of the hieroglyphics held up before them.

But he could not shut his ears to the call of others who wanted and needed the Good News. After six months helping in this way, he went to another village higher up the mountain to preach and teach.

He was about sixteen years of age by this time, and eager to be baptised. The missionary and the elders of the church at the mission station gave him a thorough examination on his knowledge of the way of salvation, of other Scriptural truths, and evidence was sought as to whether his daily behaviour was consistent with the profession he made. Having satisfactorily passed this ordeal, he went to the mission station where he was baptised, and, as usual took a new name—Yona.

He remained there for further education. It was only for one more year, and then he went back to his native hills and preached and taught there for a further four years. Eager to go further, he was then appointed to teach at a small centre close to Mwenda so that he could teach part time, and for the rest of the day go to the station school for the third year of his primary education. This was the minimum requirement for entrance to the Evangelists' School.

When he had successfully completed this year, he went to Blukwa for two years of Bible training to prepare him for the work of evangelist. He did well, and not only gained a better understanding of the Word of God, but grew in spiritual stature.

Great was the excitement when he returned to his own station of Mwenda on completion of the course, and greater still was the welcome he received when he went back once again to his home. His mother had by now come to the Lord, and his brother was already shaping for the Lord's service.

The church elders appointed him to oversee the work of a large district, helping the evangelists and encouraging the Christians. His wise and gracious way gave him great favour in the eyes of all, and when an acting pastor was needed for the church on the Mission station he was chosen. It became obvious that the Lord had marked him out for special service, and after a year as pastor on the station, he was sent to the pastors' course at Adi. This station was over four hundred miles away from Mwenda, in a different language area, and where the staple diet was different from that to which he had been accustomed.

The course was more advanced than the one he had taken previously, and was aimed at preparing the pupils for positions of leadership. Yona struggled with the unaccustomed food, and with the studies. But he did well, and finished the course with flying colours. Once again, with great joy he returned to his home country, and was given a greater welcome than ever. He was reinstated as pastor at Mwenda. After two more years of faithful and appreciated service, his name was sent to the leaders that he might be licensed to minister the sacraments, with a view to eventual ordination. He was called before the appropriate committee of missionaries and senior pastors, and given a thorough examination regarding his doctrinal views and knowledge of the Scriptures. From this ordeal he emerged successfully, and the committee recommended that he be licensed—the youngest man to be recognized in this way in our Congo field.

He is now pastor over the district in which his home is. The Lord is greatly using him. The work is flourishing in his hands, and he is greatly loved.

From the centre opened up as a result of the apparently trivial accident of a missionary taking the wrong path, no fewer than thirty-six people have gone out as teachers and evangelists in the service of the Lord Christ.

CHAPTER V

THE AZANDE TRIBE

1. Fast Bound in Sin and Nature's Night

TAP, tap, tap, tap, tap, tap, tap. The sound comes from the long grass not far from an Azande village. The man is sitting on a low stool tapping with a stick on a small piece of wood raised on twigs above the ground. For some days he has been preparing himself for the rite by strictly observing the taboos, eschewing all unworthy behaviour and practising strict self-discipline.

He prays: 'Oh, Bengi, Bengi, Bengi. You have all wisdom, all knowledge and understanding. There is nothing hid from you. You are humble and sit on the ground, while the chiefs sit on the chairs (A parable meaning that you allow the chiefs to appear to rule, while you are the true ruler). You have revealed all secrets to my father, my grandfather, and all my ancestors in the past. You have always been dependable, and there is nothing you do not know. Now, Bengi, as my ancestors have always been directed aright by you in time past, please, please reveal this matter to me.'

Information may be sought on any matter in which guidance is needed, such as taking a wife, making a new house or village, or going on a journey. The prayer is the same in each case except for the questions which naturally vary according to the circumstances.

'Now, Bengi, as you look into the future and as you see all things that will happen, as you have perfect knowledge and understanding, look over the place from which I have pulled this bunch of grass. Now, Bengi, tell me, if I were to build my compound there, would I prosper? Would my wife be healthy? Would I have children? Would my crops grow well?

'Oh, Bengi, Bengi. We know that it is a small matter for you to look out and see all this. Now, please, don't lose patience with me for asking you to tell me. Don't be angry, but please, Bengi, let me know what is going to happen. I am not dictating to you, Bengi, but if the answer to all these questions is in the affirmative, please show it by killing this chicken.'

He places a few drops of water mixed with the bark from the Bengi vine in the chicken's mouth. Very shortly after, the chicken has a convulsion and dies.

He then repeats the prayer again until he comes to the last part which he changes:

'Please, Bengi, don't be annoyed. I am not questioning your truthfulness, but this is an important matter to me. Please confirm this by letting this chicken live.'

He administers the draught exactly as before, but this time the chicken drinks it without any apparent effect.

The prayer is then repeated a third time, with special emphasis on the request that Bengi be not irritated because of the continual questioning. The praise is more lavish, and the question is asked with still greater humility. The question asked this time is a check, and is such that the true answer is obvious to all. Bengi is then requested to kill the chicken if the answer is in the negative, but if otherwise to let the chicken live. The purpose of this question is to see if Bengi is telling the truth. If the answer is incorrect, it is obvious that Bengi has been offended because the man's life is not worthy, some taboo has been broken, or he has not observed all the rules of self-denial required of those who would approach Bengi.

From the biggest chief to the lowest subject, all believe in Bengi—God's gift to them to reveal the future—and their whole lives are governed by it. One of the most important chiefs declined an invitation to go to Belgium by air because Bengi told him he should not go.

The taboos referred to are much the same in all African tribes. The tribe is divided into clans, each of which is associated with a particular animal, into which they believe they are reincarnated after death. Contact with that animal is taboo to the clan, and its flesh must not be eaten under any conditions. It is believed that that is a cause of leprosy.

Bengi is perhaps the greatest hindrance to the progress of the Gospel in the Azande tribe. In addition there are the usual accompaniments of animism—offerings to ancestors placed in the hut which could be seen in all villages; sacrifices to various spirits in the case of illness; the belief that all disease and death is caused by poison or cursing; the cult of the witchdoctor who is credited with supernatural powers, or, at anyrate, with being in touch with the unseen world and able to invoke the intervention of occult forces.

The standard of morals among the Azande is very low. Chastity is by no means regarded as a virtue, although adultery is condemned. Unfortunately the low morals are said to be due to the advent of the white man. Before that, it is said, morals were high; but the advent of the European introduced promiscuity which has remained among the tribe. In the old days, if a man was found in adultery, hands and other organs were cut off. Some of those who so suffered may still be seen.

Members of the Azande tribe may be found all over Congo and far beyond its borders. They are employed as chauffeurs and mechanics and are found in other skilled manual occupations. Some have reached Belgium, and others have wandered as far afield as New York.

It is, therefore, all the more surprising to travel round their villages and to find that in many respects they have not moved forward with the times as have most other tribes. They are in a kind of backwater. The desire for education, while growing, has not yet become a torrent, carrying all before it; and political propaganda has not made the impression upon them that it has in other parts. They are only now beginning to awake from the sleep of ages.

The reason for this is to be found partly in their innate pride. The tribe has a history of conquest. In its migration from the north it overcame and absorbed numerous less virile tribes. The assimilation of these has resulted in the tribe being a conglomeration of mixed physical characteristics. Some are light-skinned, others as dark as skins can possibly be, and between them are all shades and gradations. There are those with the coarsest negroid features, and others with finely cut Arab profiles. Here and there one finds a phenomenon uncommon among other tribes of this country—red-headed people.

Of the absorbed tribes, little trace can be found except in tradition and facial characteristics. Their languages are forgotten except by a few very old people; and *Pazande*, the tribal language of the Azande —is spoken throughout.

Their chiefs have great power. All property, animals, and fish in the rivers belong nominally to the chief, and he has a right over all the women in the tribe. Polygamy is common. One chief possessed three hundred and sixty wives, many of whom he could not recognize if he saw them, let alone know their names. Another, asked the size of his harem, replied 'Does one count the blades of grass?'

The bride-price among this tribe is very low, an indication of the low esteem in which women are held. As a consequence separation and divorce are very common. Owing to the low moral standards and the prevalence of venereal disease, the birth-rate is very small, although in recent years it has shown some improvement.

In the Azande tribe there are many secret societies one of which is known as *Bili*. This is a society which has much in common with freemasonry. It has its initiations, its rituals, its secrets, and its officers who are installed with due ceremony. Those who are not members of this movement stand in fear of it. When death comes to a member of *Bili*, he must only be buried by members of the society.

All these factors combine to make the Azande people hard to reach with the Gospel message. They are proud and self-satisfied. They have implicit faith in Bengi and in their animistic beliefs. Low moral standards mean that life is easy-going. The productiveness of the soil results in abundance of food and grain from which they make their beer. Drunkenness is very common.

Yet withal these people are kind, hospitable and generous. The greatest reproach which can be cast at anyone is that of stinginess.

This great tribe, numbering over a million, has throughout the years presented a problem to the messengers of the Cross. Dungu mission station was opened as far back as 1912, yet the ground has seemed hard and the results meagre. Promising leaders have so often fallen into gross sin.

Nevertheless the unremitting prayer which has been offered for this outstanding people has not been without its results. Even in this unpromising soil the Gospel has brought forth its fruits. Lives have been changed and churches have been brought into being in the areas covered by the five stations of the Africa Inland Mission in the tribe. The following pictures tell of some who were 'fast bound in sin and nature's night,' but have been made 'free indeed' through the great Deliverer. God's grace is undeterred by obstacles and is sovereign.

2. MBARAZA

A white man! At Dungu! Yes, they had heard of those people whose skins were white, although some who had seen them said that they were really more pink than white. Many, however, had never set eyes on them, although occasional Government officials had come round the countryside. But these were missionaries who had come to settle at Dungu on a hill near the river.

'Let's go and see them, boys!' The idea was a good one, and appealed at once to African lads, who are just as curious as those in other countries. Mbaraza responded too, and they all prepared to start on the twenty-five mile walk on the morrow.

'Yes, you may go,' said Mbaraza's father, 'but you are not to stop there.' He wouldn't have any child of his caught in the spell of these strange people from a far country; but there was no harm in the lad going to have a look at them. Indeed, it is doubtful whether his father could have succeeded had he tried to forbid him going.

The way was long, and it seemed as if the winding bush path would never end. But their enthusiasm drove them on, and at long last they found themselves climbing the one hill to be seen for miles, and approaching the mud huts which the missionaries had erected there. They gazed at them with enquiring eyes. These people must be immensely wealthy! There were all kinds of wonderful possessions to be seen. Whoever saw such pots and pans as they had for cooking their food?

And there were the white people themselves, clad in khaki, with huge hats on their heads! Yes, they were more pink than white; and their faces were different too. They looked and looked, saying little at the time, but taking everything in. They were scared, however, when the white man turned to them and greeted them in their own tongue. He invited them to come and live on the station to hear what he had come to teach them about God, and about His Son Jesus Christ who had died to save them. If they would like it, he could give them work to do so that they could earn some pocket money. They would then be able to attend school daily and learn to read for themselves.

The idea appealed to Mbaraza. He would like to have some money to spend. It would be useful, too, to learn to read. So, in spite of all his father's injunctions, he decided to stay. And to his surprise and delight, before long he was employed to wash those pots and pans he had admired so much.

God had had His eye on the lad. These things had not happened by chance. The divine potter was shaping a vessel for His use. As the lad attended school daily, and as he scrutinized the missionaries, he not only heard the Gospel, but he saw something of it displayed in the lives of these people from another land. Something began to happen, and one day he took the decisive step of coming to the Saviour about whom he had heard. He would follow Jesus.

Before long promotion came his way. He was taken off the menial task of cleaning the pots to work in the house of the missionaries. How he trembled as he handled those plates and cups. When one slipped from his hands and broke into a thousand pieces, he was very fearful of the anger of his European master. But he was reassured when the missionary simply smiled and told him he must be more careful in future.

Mbaraza attended all the meetings, and listened diligently to all the teaching which was given. There was one meeting in the week which interested him greatly. At that gathering, opportunity was given for anybody who wished to give a word of testimony, or to make confession of wrongdoing and ask for prayer. But Mbaraza had never taken part. He did not know how to frame a testimony; but surely he ought to confess something, as so many others had done. So at last he rose to his feet and confessed that he had stolen. He was asked to remain behind to be dealt with. He was asked what he had stolen. He replied that when the missionaries had thrown out the chicken bones at the end of their meal, he had taken them and licked the remains of meat he found on them!

After long instruction in the Catechism class, the

time came when he was deemed ready for baptism. He took the name of Enoka (Enoch).

God had been planning for him in other ways too. Shortly after the arrival of the missionaries at Dungu, a most unusual tragedy had taken place—a man had committed suicide, leaving three young daughters. Theirs was a perilous position in view of the low moral standards and customs of the tribe. So the Belgian official stepped in and handed them over to the mission for care and protection. They were admitted to the Girls' Home at the mission, and were brought up carefully in the ways of God. They attended school and were taught to read. Sheltered from heathen environment and brought daily under the sound of the Gospel they responded, and each for herself made a profession of faith in the Saviour. When the time came for the eldest to be baptised, she took the Biblical name of Susanah.

Enoka Mbaraza had now reached the age when a young fellow looks for a wife. 'Be ye not unequally yoked together with unbelievers,' said the book he had learned to read and to obey. He looked round for a girl who was a believer. Thus he found that, being in the way, the Lord led him to Susanah. In due course they were married, and the Lord blessed them with three daughters. The coming of children rejoiced their hearts, since so many marriages among the Azande are childless.

Shortly after their marriage they offered to go out as evangelists. They were appointed to a preaching centre, and there they gave bold and consistent witness to the reality of their trust in God. They enjoyed the work, and rejoiced in the blessings God had showered on them. There were, however, dark hours for them.

They must discover for themselves the 'treasures of darkness.' All had gone well with them, when one day somebody rushed up to their house to tell them that their eldest daughter, little six-year-old, had been accidentally drowned in the nearby stream. She had been playing there with some of the schoolboys when it happened. This was a terrible blow for the two parents, who delighted so greatly in the children the Lord had given them. Curious eyes looked on to see how they would behave. Heathen grief is so hopeless and uncontrolled. The chief mourner has often to be restrained by force lest he or she do harm to themselves while the death-wail is sounding with its despairing notes. But to the surprise of the onlookers, these two brave souls remained calm and self-possessed—nay rather, God-possessed—in the midst of their sorrow. No wailing came from their lips, or was permitted by them; and if silent tears flowed it was because of the sorrow of the bereavement, but not of despair or rebellion. 'The Lord gave, the Lord hath taken away. Blessed be the name of the Lord.' Their behaviour at that time made a deep impression on all the people. Truly the Gospel had made these people different from their neighbours. They had found a secret which the heathen did not possess.

The hand of God still led them on, and later they were sent to the evangelists' school at Aba for two years of Bible training. It has been found at home that theological studies may become deadening to the spirit, and enthusiasm is dampened. But not so with them. Enoka embraced every opportunity which came his way of heralding the good news and seeking to bring others to find the salvation he had found. Among those who found Christ there under the ministry of this student was a little Kakwa lad, whose skin and heart had been as dark as his name—Mude, which means Night. Little did his spiritual father realize the importance of that occasion. The one whom he was thus instrumental in leading to the Saviour went on in the knowledge of God and in spiritual experience to become the much-used pastor of the Aba church.

Their two years at the evangelists' school completed, they returned to Dungu, and were again sent out to be in charge of a centre in the bush. Having profited from their improved knowledge of the Word, they were able to do a deeper work than before, and to give better instruction to the converts. Thus it came about that when, some years later, a pastor was needed for the church at the mission station he was called to the post. He was a wise counsellor, faithful in all his duties, and eternity alone will reveal how great blessing resulted from his labours there.

But his earthly course was nearing its end. Bilharzia, the incidence of which is nearly one hundred per cent in many parts of Central Africa, affected him. Again and again he endured the drastic treatment, but again and again the disease reappeared. In the end it was too much for the weakened body, and Susanah was called to stand by as her devoted husband crossed to the other side.

The patient training and discipline given to their daughters has borne fruit. Each has married a devoted Christian man. One went with her husband to Aba and trained as an assistant nurse, and they are now doing medical work at Dungu. Both daughters have young families, and they are seeking grace to bring them up as they themselves were, in the nurture and admonition of the Lord.

Susanah, now a grandmother, may still be mistaken for a much younger woman. In Africa the women often age quickly, and some who are twenty years younger than Susanah often appear to be twenty years older than she. It is not that hers has been a life free from trial and care, but she has found the secret of casting all her cares upon the great Burden-bearer, and the years lie lightly upon her.

3. THE HAMMER

Whether or no the child's head resembled in some respect the shape of a hammer, or whether there was some other reason, the mother called her newborn son 'Bande'—hammer. Little did that mother know how apt the name would be, and how exactly it would suggest the persistence and perseverance which have since characterised him.

He grew up as most other Azande lads, into all the scrapes and adventures of a normal boy. Hunting, trapping and similar pursuits kept him occupied in the dry season, and the gardens kept him busy at other times. With all the others he entered into the loose promiscuous life of the tribe, and at last settled down in his own home with his wife. Later he took a second wife.

Cases of sudden conversion are rare in Africa. The Gospel message must usually be repeated again and again before any response is apparent. Sometimes a person will make profession of conversion repeatedly. Each of these expresses desire, or perhaps response to gradually increasing apprehension of the truth.

But Bande's case was an exception. The very first time he heard the Good News—away back in 1922—the Holy Spirit led him to immediate decision. He was very ignorant of the things of God, and quite illiterate, yet he seemed to grasp at once something of the implications of the step he had taken, and sought to bring his whole life into conformity with them.

The first and greatest hurdle he had to overcome lay in the fact that he had two wives. The lowered moral standards in that tribe have resulted in a very low birthrate. Many of the women are barren. So the matter was not complicated, as such cases often are, by the presence of children who have to be provided for. The inconsistency of having two wives, however, became immediately apparent to him. Promptly obedient to the light given to him, he put away his second wife. Divorce and separation are very common among the Azandes, and there was no difficulty about him doing this, and no stigma attached to it.

Responsive as he thus was, it was not long before further light was given to him. He realised that this new found faith and the joy which emancipation and salvation had brought must not be kept to himself. He must bear witness to others. But how? He was quite untaught, and letters were meaningless to him. He could not read the Word of God to the people. With ingenuity born of the Holy Spirit he procured from the missionaries pictures illustrating Bible stories, and charts showing the letters of the alphabet. He studied the pictures and learned the stories they illustrated. Then he set out to walk around in the villages explaining the pictures which he carried before him as placards, preaching the Gospel to all and sundry. He gathered the children together, and holding up the chart of letters before them, would persuade someone who knew enough to distinguish one sign from another to teach the children. They would chant them until they knew them by heart.

That was many years ago. There are schools now where the children can be taught by trained teachers, so there is not the same need as there once was for that side of the ministry. But he still maintains the practice, and this whets the appetite of the young to attend the schools.

He still carries on his witness by means of the placards. The Azande country is flat and hot. But nothing stops this man from going round on foot, carrying his precious pictures and charts. He goes to a centre and remains there for a time, preaching the Gospel to individuals or groups as the Lord opens the way. When there is a little nucleus of believers there, he asks the church to send out a resident teacher-evangelist. When this takes place, he feels that his task is finished in that place, and he makes his way to another centre where no witness exists.

How apt his name! He keeps on hammering away until he makes his impression. When he was baptised he took the additional name of Abraham. This name also is particularly suited to him, for he goes forth by faith, and as he has been blessed, so he is made a blessing to others. He travels over wide areas, trudging over sun-baked paths, indefatigably bearing witness to the One Who loved him and gave Himself for him. He says he is a needle. Just as a needle pierces the hole that the thread may follow, so he feels called to open the way for more permanent witness. He has thus been instrumental in making the initial hole in a number of places which have since developed into churches.

He is an old man now, and it has recently been discovered that he has a mild form of leprosy. He also suffers from cataract. But in spite of these physical handicaps he still goes on faithfully distributing tracts, showing his pictures, preaching the Gospel and dealing with individuals. In this he is fearless and persistent, while at the same time tactful and acceptable. He will not hesitate to bring the claims of God before heathen chief or European. Once he has begun his attack he hammers on, true to his name, keeping his prey in conversation for an hour or several hours as he deals successive blows. He is not satisfied until he succeeds in winning souls, bringing them out of bondage through faith in Jesus Christ. Great shall be his reward in heaven.

CHAPTER VI

THE PYGMIES

1. THE DWARFS OF THE MOUNTAINS OF THE MOON

DRIVING along one of the gravel roads which have been cut through the great Ituri forest with its impenetrable undergrowth, the car rounds a bend and there stands a strange miniature of a man. His skin is pale chocolate in colour. Although his frame is small, and he stands no more than four feet six inches high, his body is perfectly formed and well developed. His clothing usually consists of a strip of barkcloth. He is very shy, as are all of his race, and remind one of the gazelles of the forest, with soft large eyes. Indeed, the other tribes consider them to belong to an inferior race. One of our missionaries once heard an intoxicated pygmy walking through the forest shouting at the top of his voice, 'I'm not a pygmy; I'm a human being, I am.'

These little people are no new discovery. The ancient Greeks knew about them, although they regarded them as legendary figures living beyond the sources of the Nile and fighting the cranes and other large birds of that region.

But long before this the Egyptians of the IVth dynasty had had proof of their existence. When an Egyptian army returned to their own beloved land after an expedition of exploration in the dark 'country of spirits,' Central Africa, they brought back with them a strange captive. The reigning Pharaoh heard of it, and sent orders by special messenger that every precaution should be taken to preserve this captive alive—for he was none other than a pygmy. A bas-relief has been discovered wherein figures one of this dwarf-like race.

The memory of this strange captive was still held during the long ages of ignorance which shrouded the knowledge of the centre of the continent, and ever and anon the question arose as to whether such a race still existed.

It was not until 1870 that Schweinfurt rediscovered the pygmies. And today they exist much the same as they must have lived centuries ago, although in some respects the coming of a measure of civilization and the advent of sightseeing tourists have had some effect upon them.

Children of the forest indeed. They share its secrets which are so often hidden from others. They know the secret haunts of the forest buffalo, and of the timid and retiring okapi. With their miniature bows and arrows they are deadly shots.

One of our missionaries was tramping through the forest glades with some pygmies when he heard the song of a bird. 'Where is that bird?' he asked. 'There it is,' said one of the pygmies, pointing with his finger. But the missionary was unable to see it. 'There, at the top of that tall tree.' Still it eluded the missionary's gaze. 'There,' said his informant, and raising his bow and fitting an arrow he let it fly and brought the little songster down at the missionary's feet.

It was not many years ago when the first okapi was captured. But to the despair of the white man, he could not be persuaded to eat. In vain they sought to tempt him with choice leaves from the forest. At last it was a pygmy who informed the white man that the okapi never eats from the ground, but only from the trees. Gathering some forest leaves, he tied them in bundles high off the ground, and the animal began to eat his first meal in captivity.

Each clan of pygmies is under the overlordship of a clan of one of the forest tribes. There is an understanding between them. The overlords supply spears and hunting dogs, and in return have certain rights over the pygmies associated with them; at times they illtreat them, but on the whole the arrangement is an amicable one. The pygmies never dig gardens, but spend their time in hunting, trapping and fishing. When they need grain, they take meat to the village of their overlords and bring away grain in exchange.

The pygmies are nomadic, moving over a large area, but returning to the same part within the year. Their houses are of the most primitive type—a few branches of trees tied together, covered roughly with leaves. The furniture inside is marked by its absence. They sleep on the ground, with just a mat under them. Few have the semblance of a blanket.

They are restless, and constantly on the move. In recent years, with the coming of convoys of tourists with their largesse, many pygmy clans have set up their huts near the roads, so as to be easily accessible.

Difficult as has been the task, much has been done to bring the Gospel message to these despised people. Medical and surgical treatment has brought many of them to the mission hospitals, and regular visitation in their homes has been a means which has been used to gain their confidence. Many of them have learned Gospel choruses and texts, and have listened to Gospel records so often that they can repeat them by heart.

The good seed has been sown. Some has fallen on good ground, bringing forth fruit.

In one place a diminutive pygmy chapel has been erected where undersized people sit on undersized seats to listen to the preaching of the Word of God.

2. RESERVED ACCOMMODATION

The pygmy was ill, very ill. His whole body shook with repeated rigors and a high temperature. It had started so suddenly. He had been out in the forest with the evangelist, and without warning the illness was upon him.

They carried him to the pygmy camp to which he belonged, and all the little villagers crowded round him with concern. He felt as if everything would fall on him.

The first thought of his relatives was to send for the witchdoctor. He would sacrifice a chicken and divine the cause of the illness and how it could be remedied. But to the surprise of all, the patient refused. 'I am a Christian,' he cried, 'and I will have nothing to do with witchdoctors again.'

Whoever heard of such a thing! The height of folly! Refusing the kindness of those who would pay highly for the services of the witchdoctor! And who else could discover the reason for such an illness? Preposterous.

The pygmy prayed, weak and ill as he was. But in spite of that his illness increased and his strength waned. His relatives began to wail—the hopeless, despairing wail of heathenism.

'I am dying,' he said.

Just then he saw a bright light shining, and seemed to be transported to another place. It was a town where there were many buildings, surrounded with an unearthly radiance.

A man in shining white garments approached and talked with him. He knew it was the Lord. He conducted him round the city, and at last they came to a beautiful building. 'See,' said the Lord, 'this one has your name on it.'

'Ah,' said the pygmy, 'let me go inside and sit down; for I am tired.'

'No,' said the Lord, 'not yet. You may not enter now. First you must go back and tell people about this beautiful city, and they must believe in Me in order to have a place in it.'

With that the vision ended. He called for water; and still more water. His rigours ceased. He became conscious of the wailing of his friends.

'Why are you mourning?' he asked. 'I am alive. I have been told to come back and tell you all that you must accept the Lord as Saviour.' And he told them what he had seen.

Before long he recovered his strength, and since then he has diligently followed the Lord.

After some time his enthusiasm waned, and he grew slack in witnessing to others. One day there was a sudden storm and he was struck by lightning and nearly killed. He took it as a rebuke from God for his lack of zeal.

Since that day, many have come to the Lord through his ministry. His wife and all his living children have professed conversion, as well as many in his clan.

3. As We Forgive

There are strong family ties among the pygmies. Parents are very fond of their children, and there is more fellowship between husband and wife and children than among some other tribes. It is the usual custom with others that the women and girls eat separately from the men and boys. But the families are much more accustomed to share their meals among the pygmies.

A mission station was opened in the depths of the forest especially to reach the pygmies. It was difficult of access, and for many years the only way to reach it was by a long circuitous road through the forest, and the crossing of the final river by a swing bridge of vines suspended from the trees made by the pygmies.

On this station came a pygmy man with his wife and children, and sought permission to live there. This was gladly granted. They heard the Word of the Truth of the Gospel, and in due time came to the Saviour and received Him. The father was eventually baptised and was known as Noa (Noah) Mangala.

There were other believers among the pygmies also. One man, called Mwaka, was friendly with them, and very fond of the children, particularly of one little boy whom they named Obede (Obed).

Obede developed a boil, and Mwaka looked after him. While he was there in Noa's compound looking after the boy, the mother turned to him and said that she had heard that he had fallen into sin with a certain woman. Mwaka was indignant at the accusation, and lost his temper. He picked up a knife and threw it at the woman. It missed her, went over her shoulder and caught Obed in the neck. To Mwaka's intense sorrow, the child bled to death.

As soon as the news of the tragedy was known, Mwaka was arrested and taken to the Government post. There he was tried and imprisoned for three years.

But the matter was not over when the three years were finished, for native custom insisted that blood should be shed in revenge for the death of the child. In the ordinary way, Mwaka's life would be in danger when he returned to his clan.

Not in vain, however, had Noa learned of Christ. He was expected to revenge the life of his child, and everybody was astounded when he said that he realised that it was an accident, and that he was going to forgive Mwaka as God had forgiven him.

Forgiveness was complete, and Noa and Mwaka are firm friends. The latter is now a member of the Catechism class, preparing for baptism.

His behaviour during his three years imprisonment was exemplary, and before the Belgian Administrator Mwaka witnessed a bold confession.

Noa is one of the main pillars of the church on his station.

4. Secret Idols

The old pygmy had heard the message of God's love and His readiness to save all who accepted Christ. Again and again he had refused to commit himself. He did not yet understand. He would like to hear more before deciding. Some other time . . .

As in the case of most people who make excuses, there was a hidden reason. Hidden away among his most treasured possessions was a bag of charms. To the uninitiated, they looked like worthless rubbish. There were several teeth of animals, the claw of a certain wild bird, and a whistle which, if placed in the nostril of a dying animal and blown by his expiring breath, would bring good luck in future hunting. There were other strange things too. He knew that if he trusted

Christ he would have to part with these, and he could not face that.

But the time came when he could no longer resist the wooing of the Spirit. In a Gospel meeting he stood and before his fellows made confession of his faith. At the close of the meeting the church leaders dealt with him and counselled him.

'Of course, if you are really following Christ you will have to get rid of your bag of charms and fetishes.'

'Yes,' said he, rather hesitatingly, 'but will not some calamity overtake me if I part with them?'

He was assured that God in whom he had put his trust would protect him from the spirits, and he need not fear.

Moving in the right direction, but possibly still playing for time, he called for a fire.

It was brought, and blazed before him.

He entered his hut to bring out the bag. It seemed to be hard to find, and to take a long time. But at last he emerged with it.

He turned to the lady missionary who was there, and asked her to burn the bag and its contents for him.

She declined. It was his, and he himself must put it in the fire.

Then he turned to the evangelist, and asked him to throw the precious possession in the fire.

But he also refused.

At last, summoning all his courage, the old man cast the bag and its valued contents into the fire, and stood by as the flames consumed them.

Thus he broke with the past which had enchained him. The Son had made him free, and the old pygmy was free indeed.

Thus emancipated from the things which would

hinder him, he has made good progress in the things of God ever since.

* * * * *

Today, there is a Church among the pygmies, with meeting places scattered through the great forest. There are praying pygmies, witnessing pygmies, and one or two evangelists. The African Church in other parts of Congo sends workers among these little people. In one area, some sixty clans are known and visited. No-one really knows how many there are, and thousands are still in spiritual bondage.

CHAPTER VII

HOW GREAT A MATTER A LITTLE FIRE KINDLETH!

IT was the dry season. The hardened ground cracked open as the pitiless sun sucked every last drop of moisture from it. The long grass dried from the fresh green of the previous months to a dull lifeless brown. The air was heavy with haze. Now was the time to clean off the earth by bush fires.

Groups of men and boys could be seen going out with their bows and arrows and spears. Others went with the hunting nets. These they stretched along a broad front, while fires were started which in the high wind of the dry season would carry the flames towards them. The startled animals awakened to frenzy by the heat and crackle of the fires rushed madly to excape, only to find themselves caught in the nets, and killed by the waiting hunters.

As night fell the lights of innumerable fires could be seen from the elevation on which stood the mission hospital, and the evening breeze brought fragments of burnt grass which drifted down around the little group of missionaries watching the fascinating sight.

As they watched fires sprang into being nearer at hand. Firebrands were applied to the dried grass on the main hill of the mission station and before long the whole hill was ablaze. Strategically placed clusters of men waited with branches of trees to beat out the flames should they stray out of bounds. The fire crackled and growled fanned by the wind, and reduced the hill to a black mass covered with a pall of smoke.

How great a matter a little fire kindleth! Bushfires have been known to rage onwards for miles, burning houses and people and doing untold damage until stopped by the width of a river. When a fire is lighted, who can foretell where its effects will end?

But that evening saw the kindling of a little fire whose effects should be much more unpredictable than the dry season burnings.

That night, in that hospital, a babe was born. How many babies are born every day throughout the year, the statisticians can tell us. Many are born daily in Africa, and a large proportion do not survive the first few days of existence. But this child was unusual. She was a missionary child—a white baby born in black Africa. A few months before the mother had been desperately ill away on the lonely pioneer station in the long grass. It was a miracle that her life had been spared, and a greater miracle that a live healthy babe was born.

Before long the mother returned to that little place in the bush, bringing the precious babe in her arms. The direct route was along native paths involving four days of travel in the exhausting heat of the burning sun, carried in a carrying chair on the heads of porters. There was, however, another way. A motor road had recently been opened which went by a circuitous route to a station some fifty miles the other side of their destination. A lorry was leaving on the laborious two-hundred-mile journey and the mother climbed into it with the little bundle of preciousness. The going was rough, the accommodation was far from comfortable, but at anyrate it would save those terrifying days of exposure to the heat.

It was an exhausting trip, and when eventually they reached the end of the truck-ride, it was necesary to rest before they could contemplate facing the last fifty miles, two long days in the relentless sun.

During that interval of rest, an intrepid fellow-missionary conceived a daring plan. He had a motor-cycle and sidecar. Although there was no motor road connecting them with the little bush post, there was an African path which was wider than most. If someone else would come with him to help him over the streams, he would take the mother and baby in the sidecar in an attempt to reach their home. It was an unusual sight as they set out the next day, the missionary on his motor-cycle, another sitting behind him, the mother in the side-car, and, tucked away in the point of it, the precious bundle of new life. Between the cycle and the sidecar they carried two long planks which they could place over places difficult to cross.

Some hours later, they drove triumphantly up to the mud hut which was home to the pioneers.

The curious Africans came rushing round. A *piki-piki* away in the wilds! Few of them had seen such a thing before, the roar of its engine delighted them! They were so taken up with it that they did not notice the greater surprise until the missionary-mother produced her treasure from the depths of the sidecar. A baby! A white baby! They had never seen such a thing! The Belgian official who lived fifty miles away had a wife, but no children. One or two missionary couples with whom they had had some contact were childless. But here was a real live white baby!

The news travelled fast and far. Before many hours had passed it had reached the far ends of the tribe.

Before long inquisitive visitors arrived. They greeted

the Bwana and Madame. Good manners forbade them to ask bluntly if they might see the baby, so they talked about other things. Had they had a good journey? Were the people at Aba well? Etc. etc. But the missionaries knew full well what they had come for, and the Madame soon ended their suspense by producing the infant.

And then more visitors came. And more. And more. sometimes in ones or twos, sometimes in crowds. Sometimes from nearby villages. Some from twenty or thirty miles distant.

This was a new experience not only for the Africans, but for those missionaries. The people had been unresponsive. They felt no need of anything beyond the animism in which they had been brought up. The white man's message had no attraction for them. Moreover, until recently he had not been able to speak their language. To have the people crowding round was something quite new. They welcomed it, and did what they could to preach the Gospel to them.

But before many days it became an embarrassment. The baby's sleep was being disturbed all day long. She became fretful and unwell. This could not be allowed to go on! Must the people, who at long last were becoming friendly, be repelled and refused? The missionaries were faced with a dilemma.

They prayed about it.

The next morning messages were sent to the various chiefs. People passing through the station were asked to take messages to their villages. 'The baby will be on exhibition after the service on Sunday morning.'

Sunday's sun peeped up over the horizon promptly at six o'clock as it does every day in the tropics. There was a wide view from the mud hut in which the Bwana and the Madame lived. A little later as they looked out, trails of people could be seen winding their way along the narrow paths converging on the station. The service would not start for hours yet. But hundreds of people were gathering.

When the hour of the service arrived the little mud chapel was crowded out, while hundreds, unable to gain admission, sat on the ground outside.

It was a never-to-be-forgotten occasion. Many, if not most, of them had never heard the Gospel preached before. They listened intently. The cock-crowing, dog fighting, the crying of babies and the entrance of inquisitive goats failed to distract their attention.

At the close of the service, the whole congregation followed the missionary couple up to their mud house, and the baby was exhibited. It was hours before the people dispersed.

But they came again the next Sunday, and the following Sundays too. They were still interested in the white baby; but many continued to come because they had found an interest in the Saviour the white man had preached to them. They had learned of a way of release from the thraldom of the spirits which had so long enchained them. They were beginning to taste the joy of freedom.

Classes were started during the week for those who wished to have further instruction. People were urged to attend simple school in order to learn the alphabet that they might read the booklets of Scripture verses issued by the Scripture Gift Mission. Stiff, horny, gnarled hands were guided by the Madame as they sought to form the letters of the alphabet on slates.

The little fire thus lighted has continued to spread. On to the day when the first four carefully chosen

converts were baptised. On to the day when the first
deacons were chosen. To the great day when after
much prayer the beloved pastor, brought forward by
the Holy Spirit and prepared and owned by Him, was
set apart for the Gospel. The conflagration still goes
on. The church has now become seven churches, each
with its pastor and officers, and with an aggregate of
between three and four thousand members.

The time came when the building used as a church
on the station became obviously too small for the
united services. The Christians met and decided that
they would build a larger better edifice worthy of the
Gospel. All pledged their support for the project.

Plans were drawn up with the help of a missionary.
Gangs of men from different parts of the tribe came in
for a week or more at a time, to work voluntary on
making bricks and tiles. Women got busy bringing in
loads of firewood for burning them. Huge logs were
dragged in to be sawn into planks. Large sums of
money were collected for the purchase of tools and
other things needed for the building, and for the pay-
ment of the Christian bricklayers and carpenters who
would be employed for many months on the work.
Day after day as fresh kilns of bricks were burnt, long
lines of women and girls could be seen carrying loads
of bricks on their heads to the site of the church.

The work was done with the greatest care. The
house which was to be builded must be 'exceeding
magnifical.' Great pride was taken in every part.

It was a glad day when the great edifice was finally
completed and dedicated to the Lord. The church can
seat well over a thousand, African fashion. The sloping
floor permits everyone to see the preacher. When the
place is crowded, people sitting in the aisles, two

thousand have been able to find entrance. On special occasions not only is the building filled to capacity, but a further two or three thousand may be seen sitting outside, listening to the message through the open windows.

And still the work goes on. The church has sent its own missionaries to other parts where help was needed. It gives liberally to the British and Foreign Bible Society and to other causes.

The most-up-to-date information we have tells of more and more conversions, of the restoration of backsliders, and the steadfastness of the rank and file of the believers.

'Behold how great a matter a little fire kindleth!' The birth of a babe has been the visible means for the new birth of hundreds. And the end is not yet.

The babe herself is now a missionary there.

How is the blessing on this work to be accounted for, under God?

The first answer is that the people have been fed upon the Word of God, which has been systematically opened up to them, and which has found an abiding place in their hearts.

The second reason is to be found in this country, where faithful intercessors have held up holy hands in prayer to God.

8

THE INDIGENOUS CHURCH

WHAT is an indigenous church, and how is one established? An indigenous plant is one which is, or has become, native to the country in which it grows. It will continue to live there and propagate itself unaided. Similarly an indigenous church is one which has become rooted in a country and can carry on its activities there without the necessity of help from outside.

Many of the Lord's people, if asked to describe the missionary task, would answer that it is to fulfil the Great Commission. And when asked to quote that Commission would say, 'Go ye into all the world and preach the Gospel to every creature.' That, however, is only a part of it. Matthew gives the command at greater length than Mark, and says, 'Go therefore and make disciples of all nations, baptizing them in the name of the Father and of the Son and of the Holy Spirit, teaching them to observe all that I have commanded you.' This involves much more than a mere preaching of the Gospel message. Are those who have heard the good news and have been affected by it to be thereafter left to their own resources? As well leave a newborn infant without care and nourishment! The new convert needs instruction and oversight, and until a church is fully established which can do these necessary things for its own children, it is part of the missionary task. The aim of missionary endeavour is, therefore, not simply the preaching of the glad tidings of salvation and the instruction of converts, but also the gathering of them into the fellowship of churches which from the point of view of finance, organisation and reproduction shall no longer be dependent on outside help.

In the Acts of the Apostles we read of the church which the Holy Spirit brought into being after the Day of Pentecost, and which in many respects serves as a model for churches on the mission field. The book shows us in its opening page a group of cringing believers. But we have not to read many chapters before we are astounded to find that many local churches are referred to. As Paul travelled from place to place he left behind him not merely groups of converts but churches with their deacons and elders. Of necessity Paul had to leave these largely to their own resources; but they were taught to rely upon the Holy Spirit. In those days when communications were slow, it was impossible to refer every difficulty to Paul or to the Council at Jerusalem or Antioch. They had to look to the Lord for direction. Paul visited them when he could, or sent others. He kept in touch with them by letters. These things were occasional highlights; they had no such help for the greater part of the time. They carried on alone.

Yet not alone! It was the work of the Holy Spirit. We see Him at work adding to the church, multiplying its numbers, appointing officers over the churches, exercising discipline, presiding in its councils, and so making His will known that they could write, 'It seemed good to the Holy Ghost and to us.' We see Him calling out chosen workers for specific tasks, separating them and guiding them in His selected way.

The same Holy Spirit is at work today. From the

seemingly unpromising materials of heathen Africa He is building a church. He who applied the saving Word to the hearts of the elect is continuing to work. He calls out spiritual leaders, disciplines them by experiences which prepare them for His service, trains, equips and uses them.

The missionary who is co-operating in such a work must be careful lest he hinder the operation of the Holy Spirit or the development of the church. He can hinder the work of the Holy Spirit by usurping the office which is His alone. It is so easy for the missionary to pick out those who, in his opinion, seem to be likely material for leaders, give them special training, bring them into privileged relationship with himself, and place them in responsible positions. This has often been done, and it ends disastrously, either immediately or after years, bringing endless trouble in its train. They are man's choice, not that of the Holy Spirit. Leave it to God! In answer to prayer and without pressure from the missionary, He will bring forward those of His own choice. These are the ones He will bless and use.

Furthermore, the missionary can hinder the development of the church by retaining his position, imposing his will and making decisions for the church. He must train, and even force, the church and its leaders to rise to their responsibilities. Decisions regarding the suitability of candidates for baptism, of the use of the church's money and the accounting for it, the support of evangelists and pastors, the discipline of its members, etc., are the responsibilities of the church, and the missionary must not rob them of experience along these lines. He must insist on their shouldering their loads, even though they make their mistakes and act against his advice.

The establishment of indigenous churches has long been the aim of most missions in Congo. The rate of progress toward this goal has varied considerably. The Africa Inland Mission has by no means lagged behind in this matter. From very early days the converts were taught that it was their responsibility to support their own evangelists. Hundreds of evangelists have gone forth to preach the Gospel. Nobody would consider that they have been adequately supported; but such support as they have had has come from the offerings of the believers. They have not been allowed to depend in the slightest degree upon contributions from overseas.

Again from early days, the training of evangelists, and latterly pastors, has had a prominent place in the mission programme. Two years training in the Scriptures has been given to those among the evangelists who were, for the most part, already serving. They have gone out from the training schools in which this was given better furnished unto all good works. As these returned to their work, and continued faithfully in it, selection has been made among them of those worthy and able to take a further two years training in a pastors' school.

In the early days of the work in Congo most of the converts came to the mission station for employment, in order that they might avoid the opposition which they encountered in their heathen homes and at the same time receive further instruction in the things of God. In due time they were baptised and became members of the church on the station. The missionary was its first pastor and everything depended on him. Evangelists were sent out and, in due time, they gathered converts around them, often in places which were distant from the mission station. These, when baptised, became members of the station church even if they did not live there.

In later years, however, the mission station has lost a lot of its importance. Fewer have been employed there, and the number of church members living in their villages has greatly increased. Attention has therefore been directed in more recent years to the organization of village churches. Each of these has its own officers. A pastor usually serves several churches and his support is shared between them.

Come with me and let us visit one of these churches. We travel by car along the gravelled roads which take us fifty or a hundred miles from the station. In some parts the country is very flat and hot, and one can go for miles without seeing anything in the nature of a hill of any size. In other districts the road winds in and out among hills, by escarpments which are marvels of engineering, down into deep valleys, across rivers, and then up the other side. Travelling with us are African pastors. It is a privilege to have fellowship with these men. They are pleasant companions. Full of fun, teasing one another, chatting interestingly of places we pass, and recounting the Lord's doings. These men are amazing. True it is that owing to the strenuous efforts of missionaries and the invaluable ministry of the Bible Society they each have the whole Bible in a language they can understand. But they have practically nothing else. No commentaries. No reference libraries. No concordance. Yet these men astonish one by their detailed knowledge of the Scriptures, their application of them to the problems they face, their wise and spiritual counsel on committees and the holiness and consistency of their lives.

We arrive at the church. You would have passed it by, maybe. It is not conspicuous to European eyes. Simply a mud and pole building, with a thatched roof. Alight from the car and look inside. The poles which support the roof are not always as straight as they might be. The thatch has worn bare in places, and one can glimpse the sky through the holes in it—or if it be raining the rain soon finds the thin spots and pours through into the building.

'Are these the seats?' They are but poles laid on the ground in many places, or suspended in the forks of other poles inserted in the earth. And the pulpit is merely made of mud.

Do not look with too critical an eye on this place, however. We could wish that it were smarter and more attractive, that the seats were more comfortable, and the furnishings more beautiful. But, after all, these are but the fringes. The essence of a church is that these people meet to worship God, to hear His Word opened up, His Gospel preached. These do not necessitate ornate buildings. 'Where two or three are gathered together in My Name, there am I in the midst,' said the Lord. And that without regard to the style of building, or in the absence of a building, in which they meet. As long as they meet in His Name, He is there. And since the vital condition is fulfilled in these humble huts, the Lord is in the midst, and that is all that matters. Here fervent prayer is made. Hardened sinners and aggressive opponents of the truth have been changed and brought to the foot of the Cross in answer to prayers offered here. And as the Gospel of redeeming love is unfolded here, even though the preachers have little help, little training and little background, the Holy Spirit owns it, opens darkened minds and confirms the Word with signs following.

The service may not be as decorous as one would wish. It is quite common for a cock to crow in the middle of the sermon or prayer. Sometimes a dog-fight distracts attention for a few minutes, or an inquisitive goat pushes in through the doorway. Once we saw a monkey come and perch on a window ledge as we were speaking. And even in Africa babies will not be silenced.

Enter one of these rough buildings for a service. In most parts the women take a pride in keeping the place swept and clean, but their good work is soon undone by the treading of feet on the sandy ground. As the men enter the building, they leave their bows and arrows and spears outside. As is usual in Africa, the women sit on one side of the church and the men on the other. The men dress in European style, in slacks or shorts and shirt. Even in the hottest weather, some can be seen clad in an army or airforce greatcoat! And it is not uncommon in the more remote parts to see one enter wearing a suit of pyjamas. However, the more advanced Africans dress cleanly and neatly, with smartly polished shoes. Most of those who take a pride in their best clothes bring a piece of cloth with them which they spread out on the seat before they sit down.

The attire of the women is much more varied. Most of them have a dress or length of cloth with which to swathe themselves, even though it may have to be kept for Sunday use only. The gay colours and interesting patterns of these materials are most fascinating. Some display, in gaudy colours, the moon and stars, fishes, snakes, hens and chickens, shells, kettles and cooking utensils, old coronation materials with pictures of Queen Elizabeth and Prince Philip. Others there are with highly coloured lettering such as 'Cherie', 'I love you', or 'Independence.'

The singing is, in many cases, led by hornblowers, or cornettists. Some years ago an enterprising missionary started a music school. He taught the Africans to read music, and to play various wind instruments. They took to this extraordinarily well, and in many of the churches the lusty singing owes much to these men.

Should you be sufficiently curious as to open your eyes during the prayer, you might be surprised to see that as the leader is addressing God he accompanies his requests by actions, as if he were conversing with a fellow. The petitions are sometimes unconventional, but full of meaning.

'We are like a big lorry. We load everything on to it, our intentions, our desires, our sermons and all good works. But unless there is someone to drive the lorry, we get nowhere. So we need the Holy Spirit if all that we do is going to get anywhere.'

'Lord, I have noticed that if grease drops on to thick paper it soaks in and becomes one with the paper. So may Thy Word which we hear soak right into our lives and form a whole with them.'

'Lord, when our beds or our furniture get bedbugs or lice in them we put them out in the sun and all the insects go away from them. So, Lord, as we come into the sunlight of Thy Presence, chase away all the bad things from our hearts.'

'I am simply like a horn. I can do nothing of myself. Breath, tune, force and beauty come from the one who blows it.'

The sermon is simple and direct. Here is an outline of one given recently by one of the pastors.

The reading was Jeremiah 18. 1-6. The Potter at work. He described carefully the making of an earthenware pot. The clay is chosen carefully, dug out of the ground, beaten on a stone, built up painstakingly, little by little. 2 Cor. 4.7; Tim. 2.20; Psa. 119.73. Sometimes, however, the vessel is marred by little pieces of gravel left in the clay, and has to be made over again. When completed it is fired to make it hard and strong and useful.

It is made according to the desire of the potter—small or large, and of the shape he wants for his particular need. Rom. 9. 20, 21. The owner puts it where he wishes. Some are kept in one place for storing water. Others are used for cooking, and are always being placed on the fire where the heat is fierce Acts 9.15.

The Potter wants a good pot, 2 Tim. 2. 19, 21; 1 Thess. 4. 4; Eph. 2. 10.

Attention is reasonably good, although one would hardly expect unbroken concentration for a sermon of an hour or more. But they believe in giving good value for money.

At the conclusion of the service, those who desire counsel remain behind. Some wish to make profession of faith in Christ. Others have fallen into sin and wish to put things right.

How did these centres come into being? By varied means and instrumentalities. Sometimes a sick man has been to the hospital or dispensary on the mission station many miles away. There he has heard the life-giving word, has responded, and has come back with a fervent desire that others may hear also. He has persuaded his friends and neighbours to erect a hut, and a mud chapel, and to ask that an evangelist may be posted there. In other cases, the desire on the part of parents that there should be a school for their children has led to the request that a centre be opened there. On one occasion—typical of many others—a missionary was going on furlough and asked his cook what he would like to do during his employer's absence. He replied that if the Bwana would transport him and his family and belongings to his village, many miles from the mission station, he would like to open a centre there and preach the Gospel. In other cases, the church leaders have felt that a witness should be established at a strategic point. So through one or other of these means, centres have been established.

But do not think for one moment that all the church buildings are crude. The African of today is ambitious, and Christians desire to worship in buildings which shall be worthy of the Lord. In many places they have given sacrificially of their money and strength in order to provide a permanent edifice. Men, women and even children have given their labour. They have puddled mud to make bricks and tiles; have cut and carried wood to burn them; have carried them to the chosen site. Smartly dressed women have removed their shoes and have worked side by side with their poorer sisters. The help of missionaries has been enlisted in the preparation of plans, the ordering of materials and the supervision of the more difficult details of building. But the work has been carried out by the people themselves. They have worked joyfully and taken great pride in the building. The house must be 'exceeding magnifical'. Some of these churches seat as many as a thousand, and one, at anyrate, when crowded to capacity can hold double that number.

A two-year course of instruction is found advisable

before baptism. At its conclusion, the candidates are examined by a committee of elders as to their personal knowledge of the way of salvation, and of the Scriptures. The answers they give would be excellent, even if they came from the lips of well-instructed Christians in the homeland. After this, they are brought before the local church that evidence may be given as to the consistency of their lives.

It is a great occasion when the crowd gathers at the river bank (although nowadays, with the permanent buildings, a baptistry is usually built in, and the ceremony is held in the church) and the converts are immersed in the waters, confessing their faith in Christ, and their intention of walking in newness of life. These are sacred moments.

A few years ago a committee was appointed in the Congo field of our mission to re-examine our methods, and to consider whether they were wise and up-to-date, and to see that we were not getting into a rut. This, needless to say, had no reference to any change in our message, for the same Gospel is still 'the power of God unto salvation to everyone that believeth'. Among the recommendations of this committee was one that we should accelerate the pace of the organization of local churches. To further this end, the office of Church Advisor was instituted. His duty it was to travel round with some of the leading pastors to instruct the church-members as to their responsibilities, to teach the deacons and elders their duties, and to counsel the pastors, as well as to explain to all the rules and organization of the church.

To the leading pastor was committed the delicate task of giving instruction regarding the offerings. And how tactfully and wisely it was done!

'Let everyone of you lay by him in store, as God hath prospered him.'

'Has your maize borne well? Who made it do so? Who gave the rain and the sun and kept down the insect pests and animals which would destroy it? God has prospered it. Have you given a due proportion to Him?'

'What about your millet? Your groundnuts? Your sweet potatoes? Your beans? Your semsem? As God has prospered you, so give to Him.

'Have your goats done well? Your fowls? Have you had a good supply of eggs? How much have you given to God?

'Has God given you the ability to make baskets? Or mats? Or cooking pots? Or chairs? Or tables? Have you ever said "I am going to make this one for God"? And then sold it and given the money to Him? A proportion of all belongs to God for it is He Who has prospered you.'

Meet with the elders. They have difficult and complicated problems to discuss.

Here is a convert who is a polygamist. What should he do with his plural wives. The simple rule would seem to be, at first sight, to send them all away except the first. But some have borne his children? Are they to be sent away too, and thus be deprived of a father's help?

Maybe one of his later wives was converted before he was, and has been instrumental in bringing him to the Saviour. Is he to send her away, and retain his first wife who is still a heathen?

In another case there is a broken marriage. Both the man and his wife were church members, and married in church. But they had no children, and her heathen relatives persuaded her to leave her husband. Since then she has lived in sin with one man after another. He has done all he can to win her back, and has enlisted the help of others in an attempt to influence her to return; but without success. Is he to be forever without a helpmeet to look after him, to cook for him and work in the garden? Does not this expose him to too much temptation, Africa being what it is?

As they deal with these and other difficult problems, it is encouraging to note how wisely and prayerfully the teachings of Scripture are applied to each case.

Mere Europeans marvel as with the greatest of patience they ferret out the truth in the case of the disputes they have to settle. They have great wisdom along this line.

'What can be expected from people so lately out of heathenism, with so little education and Christian background?' some have asked. 'Look at the spiritual condition of many of the churches in the homeland, with centuries of Christian teaching behind them!'

We must not allow ourselves to base our expectations for the African churches on the low level of many congregations at home. Rather let us look back to the Acts of the Apostles and see what the Holy Spirit wrought in the early days of the church at Jerusalem. Since He is still in the midst of the church, let us look to Him to produce similar results in these days.

And such expectations are being justified. In the hands of spiritually-minded African leaders the work is going on and making progress. Souls are being saved, backsliders restored, and testimony is being borne to the power of the risen Lord in holiness of daily lives.

Epilogue

IT is an education for the European to go hunting with Africans. They are learned when it comes to field lore.

Rise in the early morning and go with them to the hunt. They can identify every track seen in the sand or mud, and can tell whether the animal passed last night or more recently. Then, when fresh tracks have been found, the group sets off, the tracker leading, arrow in hand with which he indicates each footprint. Across the grassland, down the steep slopes into the stream, up the other side, through the dew-soaked grass, the wet undergrowth and steaming heat, until at last the quarry is sighted.

In the preceding pages we have seen something of the divine footprints. The results brought about, the lives changed, the churches planted cannot be accounted for in the terms of mere human exertion. God has been at work. The evidence is unmistakable. Moreover, He is still working, and whatever the future may hold for Congo He will continue to work. 'He which hath begun a good work . . . will perform it until the day of Jesus Christ' (Phil. 1.6).

Uhuru—political freedom and liberation—has come to the Congolese. But what is much more important many have been liberated in the truest sense, set free from chains of sin, of superstition and of fear.

'They were bound, but Thou hast freed them.
Now they go to free the slaves.'

To them, in their turn, is committed the propagation

127

of the Gospel, the preaching of the emancipating message of Jesus Christ to those who are fettered. In Congo today many are turning to the Saviour and finding in Him salvation and release. 'The Gospel is the power of God unto salvation to everyone who believeth' whatever be the colour of the skin of the one who bears the message. 'Through your prayer, and the supply of the Spirit of Jesus Christ', the work will go on.